THOMAS JEFFERSON

The Presidents of the United States

George Washington
1789–1797

John Adams
1797–1801

Thomas Jefferson
1801–1809

James Madison
1809–1817

James Monroe
1817–1825

John Quincy Adams
1825–1829

Andrew Jackson
1829–1837

Martin Van Buren
1837–1841

William Henry Harrison
1841

John Tyler
1841–1845

James Polk
1845–1849

Zachary Taylor
1849–1850

Millard Fillmore
1850–1853

Franklin Pierce
1853–1857

James Buchanan
1857–1861

Abraham Lincoln
1861–1865

Andrew Johnson
1865–1869

Ulysses S. Grant
1869–1877

Rutherford B. Hayes
1877–1881

James Garfield
1881

Chester Arthur
1881–1885

Grover Cleveland
1885–1889

Benjamin Harrison
1889–1893

Grover Cleveland
1893–1897

William McKinley
1897–1901

Theodore Roosevelt
1901–1909

William H. Taft
1909–1913

Woodrow Wilson
1913–1921

Warren Harding
1921–1923

Calvin Coolidge
1923–1929

Herbert Hoover
1929–1933

Franklin D. Roosevelt
1933–1945

Harry Truman
1945–1953

Dwight Eisenhower
1953–1961

John F. Kennedy
1961–1963

Lyndon B. Johnson
1963–1969

Richard Nixon
1969–1974

Gerald Ford
1974–1977

Jimmy Carter
1977–1981

Ronald Reagan
1981–1989

George H. W. Bush
1989–1993

William J. Clinton
1993–2001

George W. Bush
2001–2009

Barack Obama
2009–

THOMAS JEFFERSON

TRUDI STRAIN TRUEIT

mc **Marshall Cavendish**
Benchmark
New York

Marshall Cavendish Benchmark
99 White Plains Road
Tarrytown, NY 10591-5502
www.marshallcavendish.us

All Internet addresses were correct at the time of printing.

Library of Congress Cataloging-in-Publication Data

Trueit, Trudi Strain.
Thomas Jefferson / by Trudi Strain Trueit.
p. cm. — (Presidents and their times)
Summary: "Provides comprehensive information on President Thomas Jefferson and places him within his historical and cultural context. Also explored are the formative events of his times and how he responded"—Provided by publisher.
Includes bibliographical references and index.
ISBN 978-0-7614-3622-5
1. Jefferson, Thomas, 1743–1826—Juvenile literature. 2. Presidents—United States—Biography—Juvenile literature. I. Title.
E332.79.T78 2010
973.4'6092—dc22
[B]
2008014536

Editor: Christine Florie
Publisher: Michelle Bisson
Art Director: Anahid Hamparian
Series Designer: Alex Ferrari

Photo research by Connie Gardner

Cover photo by The Granger Collection

The photographs in this book are used by permission and through the courtesy of: *Corbis:* Bettmann, 3, 68, 77, 95; David Muench, 13; George Catlin, 73; *Art Resource:* Reunion des Musees Nationaux, 84; The New York Public Library, 89; *The Granger Collection:* 6, 17, 27, 33, 39, 45, 48, 49, 51, 57, 60, 62, 72, 81, 86, 96 (R &L), 97(L); *North Wind Picture Archive:* 9, 11, 31, 43, 65; *Getty Images:* Hulton Archive, 29; *Bridgeman Art Library:* The Battle of Lexington, 19th April 1775, 1910 (oil on canvas), Wollen William Barnes (1857-1936), 23; Captain Merriweather Lewis and William Clark encountering Native American Indians, 1920 (oil on canvas) Beringhuase, Oscar (1874–1952), 75; The Burr Hamilton Duel, 1804 (coloured engraving) American School, (19th century), 78; Portrait of Thomas Jefferson 1856 (oil on canvas) Sully, Thomas (1783–1872), 91, 97(R); The Jefferson Memorial, Washington, DC built in 1943, 93; *The Image Works:* Ann Ronan Picture Library/HIP, 38; Mary Evans Picture Library, 46.

Printed in Malaysia
1 3 5 6 4 2

CONTENTS

A man of many accomplishments, Thomas Jefferson holds a prominent place in U.S. history.

YOUNG DREAMER

$\mathcal{L}$ife, liberty, and the pursuit of happiness." A mere seven words, yet they clearly defined the spirit of a country longing to be free. Thomas Jefferson wrote this stirring line as part of the Declaration of Independence, his most famous work. Since Jefferson wrote the document more than two hundred years ago, it has not lost its shine. Recently, Americans ranked the Declaration of Independence as the most influential document in U.S. history.

Even so, the Declaration of Independence is far from being Thomas Jefferson's only accomplishment. This brilliant statesman served as the nation's first secretary of state, led one of the first American political parties, doubled the size of the United States, and sent out the first federal expedition to explore the American West. Last but not least, he served as the third president of the United States (1801–1809).

A tall, striking man, Jefferson was an eager student of life. He devoured books in his quest to understand humanity and the world. Jefferson felt that "knowledge is power, that knowledge is safety, that knowledge is happiness." He found peace in books, music, farming, and family. And he held fast to these comforts when complex issues tore at him—issues such as war, slavery, and American-Indian affairs.

In his lifetime, Jefferson wrote thousands of letters and documents. The Library of Congress is home to 27,000 of them—the largest collection of Jefferson papers in the world. Soft-spoken yet driven, Jefferson let his pen become his voice. It became a voice for others, too: common citizens, a frustrated colony, a fledgling nation. In his nearly sixty years of public service, Thomas Jefferson left a legacy that few who followed in his political footsteps could match.

HAPPY CHILDHOOD

Peter and Jane (Randolph) Jefferson welcomed their third child and first son, Thomas, on April 13, 1743. Thomas Jefferson was born in a modest house at Shadwell, the family farm in the foothills of Virginia's Blue Ridge Mountains. Jefferson was born a British citizen because the United States did not exist in the mid-1700s. Virginia was not yet a state. Settled in 1607, Virginia was the first, the largest, and the wealthiest of Britain's thirteen American colonies.

Jefferson's mother, Jane, came from a noted Virginia family. Typically, such well-to-do families owned large plantations, farms spanning thousands of acres. They relied on slaves brought from Africa to grow tobacco, corn, and other crops. Jefferson's father, Peter, was not from a family of wealth. He was one of the first white settlers to put down roots in the foothills of Albemarle County, Virginia, on the frontier. He acquired more land until he owned several plantations. Peter was a talented **surveyor**. Young Jefferson wrote that his father was hired to help "make the first map of Virginia, which had ever been made."

In 1745 Jane's cousin, William Randolph, died. In his will, Randolph requested that Peter and Jane bring their family to live at his estate, Tuckahoe. He wanted them to raise his three children (his wife had died a few years earlier). Thomas's earliest childhood memory was making the journey from Shadwell in Albemarle County east to Tuckahoe. The toddler rode on horseback in the arms of a slave. The unpaved roads were so terrible that the 50-mile trip took three days to complete.

CRACKING THE BOOKS

"My father's education had been quite neglected," wrote Jefferson in his autobiography, "but being of a strong mind, sound judgment, and eager after information, he read much and improved himself." Peter Jefferson made sure his son received the education he had never had. When Jefferson was five, he joined his sisters and the Randolph children, who were taught by a tutor. Jefferson developed a great love for books. From the age of six to twenty-five, he read between ten and twelve hours each day! He devoured the works of ancient writers and philosophers, such as Homer and Socrates.

Thomas Jefferson's father ensured that his son received a proper education.

In 1752 the Jefferson family returned to Shadwell to look after the plantation. Jefferson stayed behind to attend a private boarding school. He studied Latin, Greek, and French, and he learned to play the violin.

Jefferson admired his father's strong and kind character and longed to be like him. With his reddish-blond hair, gray eyes, fair skin (he was prone to freckles), and lanky build, he certainly grew to resemble Peter. Thomas eventually reached a height of 6 feet, 2.5 inches. Father and son shared a love of nature, horses, music, and books. The pair often imagined what it would be like to explore the vast American West.

Jefferson also learned the importance of community service from his father. Peter was an officer in the Virginia **militia**. He was also an elected representative in the House of Burgesses in the Virginia legislature. The House of Burgesses crafted colonial laws under the supervision of the British-appointed governor.

The year Jefferson turned fourteen, Peter suddenly became ill and died. Young Thomas was devastated. It was the first of many such painful losses in his life. Still reeling from his father's death, he went to study with Reverend James Maury at a boarding school 12 miles from Shadwell.

When I recollect that at fourteen years of age, the whole care and direction of myself was thrown on myself entirely, without a relative or friend qualified to advise or guide me, and recollect the various sorts of bad company with which I associated from time to time, I am astonished that I did not turn off with some of them, and become as worthless to society as they were.

—Thomas Jefferson to his grandson,
Thomas Jefferson Randolph, 1808

One friend who influenced Jefferson positively was Dabney Carr. The two met at Maury's boarding school. On weekends, they rode horses at Shadwell. They often stopped to rest on a hill they had named Tom's Mountain. Jefferson told Carr that someday he planned to build a house on that very spot. The friends made a pact that when one of them died, the survivor would bury the other on Tom's Mountain. (Carr eventually married Jefferson's younger sister, Martha.) After a few years at the Maury school, Jefferson, now seventeen, was ready for a bigger challenge: college.

The Lure of the Law

In 1760 Jefferson headed to Virginia's bustling capital of Williamsburg to attend the College of William and Mary. The second-oldest college in the nation after Harvard, William and Mary was the school for Virginia's best and brightest—and richest. Jefferson took with him his personal slave, a young African American named Jupiter.

At school, Dr. William Small was one of Jefferson's favorite teachers. Dr. Small taught him math, science, and ethics. He also introduced Jefferson to influential people such as Francis Fauquier, the royal governor of Virginia, and noted attorney George Wythe.

During the mid-1700s, Thomas Jefferson attended the College of William and Mary in Williamsburg, Virginia.

An Enlightening Experience

Young Thomas Jefferson was fascinated by the Enlightenment, a revolutionary movement sweeping through Europe and America. It was tradition for people to accept what the church taught about how the universe worked. Now, they were beginning to see that sciences such as chemistry, physics, and math could unravel many of the universe's mysteries. Scientists such as Isaac Newton, who discovered gravity, were starting to explain the laws of nature.

The Enlightenment, also called the Age of Reason, was based on the views of philosophers like John Locke (1632–1704). Locke thought that people were basically honest and were shaped by their environment. He believed that ordinary citizens—not kings, the church, or wealthy citizens—were capable of running their own governments. At a time when Virginia's rich plantation owners were leading the colony, these ideas intrigued the college student with frontier roots. Jefferson had seen firsthand how pioneers, like his father, could build something from nothing. He had no doubt that ordinary citizens, when educated in Enlightenment principles, could run their own government. These ideals shaped his personal and political views for the rest of his life.

Fauquier so enjoyed Jefferson's company that he invited him to dine at his mansion regularly. Seated at the governor's glittering dinner table, Jefferson took part in lively conversations about religion, science, and world events.

Home Sweet Home

Monticello became Thomas Jefferson's most treasured possession and lifelong obsession. Construction on the house began in 1769 and continued for the next forty years as Jefferson built, added, and remodeled sections. He made more than two hundred sketches of his ever-changing plans. "I am savage enough to prefer the woods, the wilds, and the independence of Monticello, to all the brilliant pleasures of this gay Capital," wrote Jefferson while living in Paris, France.

(continued)

Monticello Facts:

- Each year, more than half a million tourists visit Monticello.

- The 11,000-square-foot house has forty-three rooms, thirteen skylights, eight fireplaces, and an alcove bed. Jefferson designed the bed to fit in the wall between his bedroom and office so he could roll out of bed into either room.

- The Temple of Vesta in Rome was Jefferson's inspiration for adding an octagonal room with a 28-foot dome in 1800. He called it the sky dome.

- Monticello is the only home in the United States on the United Nations World Heritage List of international treasures. The list includes such famous places as the Grand Canyon, the Great Pyramids in Egypt, and the Great Wall of China.

- If Monticello looks familiar it may be because it is on the "tails" side of the U.S. nickel. Jefferson himself is on the "heads" side.

When he turned twenty-one, Jefferson came into his inheritance. According to British law, the firstborn son received the majority, if not all, of the family estate upon his father's death. This was called the law of **primogeniture**. Jefferson's mother was given a "life interest" in Shadwell, but Thomas's sisters would be bound by law to turn over any land they inherited to their husbands. As the eldest of two sons, Jefferson eventually would inherit Shadwell, 5,000 acres of land, and about twenty slaves. His younger brother, Randolph, eventually got Snowden, a smaller estate on the James River. Jefferson would come to criticize the law of primogeniture. Fifteen years later, as a state legislator, he would help **repeal** it.

Jefferson set out to realize the dream he had shared with Dabney Carr. He started clearing land on Tom's Mountain to build his home. Jefferson designed the house himself. He called it *Monticello*, an Italian word meaning "little mountain." While Monticello was still under construction, a fire tore through Shadwell. Jefferson lost "every paper I had in the world and almost every book" in the blaze. He moved into Monticello earlier than he had intended. During the harsh winter of 1770, he lived in an 18-by-18-foot room.

In colonial America there were no law schools. Instead, a future lawyer studied with a professional attorney for two years. When Jefferson graduated from William and Mary, he began training with his mentor, George Wythe. He studied with Wythe for five years instead of the usual two. During this time, Jefferson often walked to the state capitol to watch the House of Burgesses in action. The debates were getting much more passionate. British policies were creating turmoil in the colonies. The storm clouds of revolution were brewing. And the shy, gentle Virginian was about to place himself directly in their path.

THE REVOLUTIONARY Two

*I*n the mid-1760s things were heating up between England and her British colonies in America. From 1756 to 1763, colonial militia had fought alongside British troops and several American-Indian tribes to drive the French and their allies out of North America. Britain now controlled nearly half the continent. But the war had been costly. Britain was in serious debt. King George III and **Parliament** thought the colonies should pay their fare share of the war expenses, as well as the costs for continuing to defend America. To raise funds, Britain began imposing taxes on the colonies—first the Sugar Act in 1764, then the Stamp Act in 1765.

On May 30, 1765, law student Thomas Jefferson was standing at the door of the Virginia House of Burgesses when delegate Patrick Henry took the floor. Henry made a dramatic speech condemning the Stamp Act.

> *[I] heard the splendid display of Mr. Henry's talents as a popular orator. They were great indeed; such as I have never heard from any other man. He appeared to me to speak as Homer wrote.*
>
> —Thomas Jefferson

Jefferson had a weak voice, and may have had a speech impediment. He admired Patrick Henry for his smooth speaking ability, but that was about all. Jefferson found Henry to be unorganized, clueless about how to write effective legislation, and "the laziest man in reading I ever knew." More than once over the years, Henry proved to be a thorn in Jefferson's side.

Patrick Henry delivers his famous speech denouncing the Stamp Act.

Tax Trouble

Under the Stamp Act, every piece of paper printed in the colonies had to be stamped, from marriage certificates to newspapers to playing cards. The tax was similar to one in Britain, and it amounted to less than what British citizens paid. Still, it angered the colonies. British citizens could only be taxed by a legislature that *directly* represented them. It seemed fair that this should hold true in the colonies, too. But the colonies were not allowed to send a single representative to Parliament. Boston attorney James Otis sounded the rallying cry, "Taxation without representation is tyranny!"

Jefferson believed that when a government was not representing its citizens properly, people had the right to change it. Throughout the 1760s the young Virginian was loyal to Britain. However, as Parliament continued levying taxes against the colonies without allowing them a voice in government, Jefferson was among many Americans who grew more and more frustrated.

The colonies decided not to import any goods from Britain until the Stamp Act was repealed. In time, Parliament caved in to pressure from British merchants and revoked the law. However, on the very same day it struck down the Stamp Act, Parliament passed the Declaratory Act. This measure gave Britain the right to make laws in the colonies "in all cases whatsoever." Two years later Parliament imposed more taxes on the colonies. Named for the British treasurer who proposed them, Charles Townshend, the Townshend Acts (1767) taxed glass, lead, paper, paint, and tea that the colonies imported from Britain. The tax was to be paid indirectly by merchants, rather than directly by the people. The new scheme was not fooling anyone.

By now, Jefferson was back in the House of Burgesses, this time as a full-fledged lawyer and newly elected delegate. Jefferson joined the majority. He voted for resolutions stating that only the Virginia legislature had the right to levy taxes in the colony. Governor Norborne Berkeley, known as Lord Botetourt, angrily responded by disbanding the entire legislature.

Most of the members of the house, including Jefferson, defied Botetourt. They met at the Raleigh Tavern. The ousted group wrote a document pledging not to import any products from Britain until the Townshend Acts were revoked. In the summer of 1769 Botetourt called for new house elections. Jefferson and most of his fellow legislators were easily reelected. Fearing a boycott, Parliament repealed all of the Townshend Acts except the tax on tea. Jefferson knew this was a warning to the colonies that Britain had no intention of loosening its grip on America, and it worried him.

A Perfect Match

In fall 1770, twenty-seven-year-old Jefferson had more than politics on his mind. He was in love. Her name was Martha Wayles Skelton. Martha's father, John Wayles, was a Virginia lawyer, plantation owner, and slave importer. At twenty-two, Martha was already a widow. Her husband had died and left her to raise their infant son, John. When Jefferson met Martha, whom he nicknamed Patty, she was living at her parents' plantation, Poplar Forest, near Williamsburg, Virginia.

The bookish Jefferson was awkward around women, but Martha's lively personality and kindness charmed him. She was an excellent musician. When Jefferson visited her at Poplar Forest, the two played music and sang together—Martha at her harpsichord and Jefferson on the violin. No known portraits of Martha exist, but family accounts describe her as "a very attractive person" and "graceful, ladylike, and accomplished." Her brother-in-law, Robert Skipworth, told Jefferson she was a woman with "the greatest fund of good nature."

In 1771 Martha's four-year-old son, John, died. Jefferson was grief-stricken. He had looked forward to being a stepfather. On New Year's Day, 1772, Thomas and Martha were married at Poplar Forest. As a blizzard swirled around them, the newlyweds moved into Monticello, which was still under construction—and would be for quite some time. That September, their first child, Martha (nicknamed Patsy) was born. Jefferson was delighted. Later, he looked back on his marriage to Martha as a time of pure joy, or what he called "unchequered happiness."

A PATRIOT'S POWERFUL PEN

May 1773 brought tragedy. Dabney Carr, Jefferson's friend, brother-in-law, and newly elected member to the House of Burgesses, died of fever. The two had just finished working in the house to pass a resolution creating the Committee of Correspondence. The committee was meant to open the lines of communication between Virginia and the other colonies as tensions with Britain grew. Carr's death deeply affected Jefferson. True to their childhood pact, Jefferson buried his friend on Tom's Mountain. Carr's was the first grave in the family cemetery at Monticello. Shortly after Carr's burial, Martha's father, John Wayles, died. The Jeffersons inherited Poplar Forest, about 135 slaves, and some large debts to banks in England. Jefferson closed his law practice to focus on running the plantations, but it was not long before politics took center stage.

On December 16, 1773, in response to the tea tax, colonial protestors in Massachusetts raided three British tea ships docked in Boston Harbor. Disguised as Mohawk Indians, the colonists dumped 90,000 pounds of British tea into the water. This event became known as the Boston Tea Party. In 1774 Parliament fired back with the Intolerable Acts. These measures closed the port of Boston, sent troops to occupy the city, and shut down the Massachusetts Assembly. King George figured he could bring Massachusetts back into line by cutting her off from the rest of the colonies. He figured wrong. The move only brought the colonies closer together.

Jefferson led the outcry in the Virginia Assembly. He proposed that June 1, 1774—the day the British were to close Boston Harbor—be "a day of fasting, humiliation, and prayer, to implore Heaven to avert us from the evils of civil war, to inspire us with firmness in support of our rights, and to turn the hearts of the King and Parliament to moderation and justice." The resolution passed without a single "no" vote. "The Governor dissolved us, as usual," said Jefferson. It did not matter. The lawmakers held a meeting of the Committee of Correspondence at the Raleigh Tavern. They wrote letters to the other colonies. They urged their fellow Americans to send delegates to a special convention, or congress, in Philadelphia.

Jefferson returned to Monticello and picked up his pen. He wrote a twenty-three-page pamphlet called *A Summary View of the Rights of British America*. It was his first major political paper. Jefferson planned to take the pamphlet to the conference in Williamsburg, where the delegates for the Philadelphia congress were to be selected. However, he became ill and had to send it on by messenger. In *A Summary View* Jefferson argued that the colonists had settled freely in America; they were not beholden to Parliament, and their allegiance to the king was entirely voluntary. As such, they were entitled to be taxed only by a legislature that directly represented them. He wrote that "the British Parliament has no right to exercise authority over us," and the colonists were "a free people claim[ing] their rights as derived from the laws of nature, and not as the gift of their Chief Magistrate. . . . Kings are the servants, and not the proprietors of the people." Jefferson said that the colonies did not want to separate from their motherland, only to gain the rights of the colonial government. He wrote, "The God who gave us life, gave us liberty at the same time." In 1774 these were strong words—too strong even for some of the colonists. The First Continental Congress, trying to avoid a violent reaction, opted to send the more subtle Declaration of Colonial Rights and Grievances to King George III. The declaration restated the colonies' grievances and announced a **boycott** of British goods. The king ignored it.

The following year, British troops were ordered to shut down the Massachusetts Assembly, arrest its members, and take control of a stockpile of colonial weapons. Warned by patriots such as Paul Revere, the Massachusetts militia was prepared for the raid. On April 17, 1775, gunfire rang out between American and British soldiers, first at Lexington, then at Concord. The American Revolution was underway.

A Summary View made a name for Jefferson in America as a superior political writer and a leader in the fight for colonial rights. When the pamphlet was published in England, it made him a target. Thomas Jefferson was earmarked as one of America's most

Artist William Barnes Wollen painted The Battle of Lexington, 19th April 1775. *This battle was the first engagement between American and British troops, and the initiation of the American Revolution.*

dangerous rebels. The British had good reason to be concerned. He was.

DECLARING INDEPENDENCE

On June 21, 1775, Jefferson arrived in Philadelphia as a delegate to the Second Continental Congress. He was pleased to meet the other representatives, among them Benjamin Franklin, Samuel Adams, and John Adams. By now, most politicians had either heard about or read *A Summary Review*. "Mr. Jefferson had the Reputation of a masterly Pen," remarked John Adams. "He looks like a very sensible spirited fine Fellow," said Rhode Island delegate Samuel Ward, "and by the Pamphlet which he wrote last Summer he certainly is one."

At the congress, Jefferson worked tirelessly. He served on thirty-four committees in just two years. Shy about public speaking, he became an expert at writing legislation. "During the whole time I sat with him in Congress, I never heard him utter three Sentences together," said John Adams. "Though a silent member in Congress, he was so prompt, frank, explicit, and decisive upon committees that he soon seized upon my heart." Jefferson was impressed with Adams's wisdom, judgment, and dynamic speaking ability. The two became good friends.

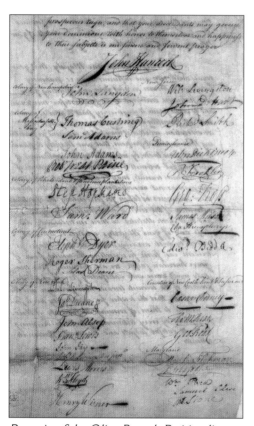

Page six of the Olive Branch Petition lists the signatures of the members of Congress who sought a compromise to settle their differences with Britain's Parliament.

In summer 1775 Congress sent the Olive Branch Petition to King George. The petition asked him to step in and settle the differences between Parliament and the colonial government before things got worse. The king not only refused, but also called the petition "traitorous correspondence," and he ordered all "loyal subjects, to use their utmost endeavors to withstand and suppress such rebellion." The gap between the two sides was growing wider.

By May 1776 the Continental Congress felt it was time to act. In June a committee was appointed to draft a resolution announcing that the colonies were splitting from Britain to form their own nation. The committee included Jefferson, John Adams (Massachusetts), Benjamin Franklin (Pennsylvania), Roger Sherman (Connecticut), and Robert Livingston (New York). In his autobiography, John Adams wrote that Jefferson suggested that Adams write the document. Adams argued that Jefferson was the best candidate because he was from Virginia, more respected by the delegates, and the best writer in the group. Jefferson remembered the occasion slightly differently, saying the committee "unanimously pressed on myself alone to make the draught." In either case, Jefferson got the job.

BIRTH OF A NATION

We hold these truths to be self-evident, that all men are created equal, that they are endowed by their Creator with certain unalienable Rights, that among these are Life, Liberty and the pursuit of Happiness.—That to secure these rights, Governments are instituted among Men, deriving their just powers from the consent of the governed, that whenever any Form of Government becomes destructive of these ends, it is the Right of the People to alter or to abolish it, and to institute new Government. . . . We, therefore, the Representatives

(continued)

of the united States of America, in General Congress, Assembled,
appealing to the Supreme Judge of the world for the rectitude of our
intentions, do, in the Name, and by Authority of the good People of
these Colonies, solemnly publish and declare, That these United
Colonies are, and of Right ought to be Free and Independent States.

—from the Declaration of
Independence, 1776

Did You Know?

• You can see the original 24 1/4-by-29 3/4 inch Declaration of Independence in the rotunda of the National Archives Building in Washington, D.C. It is on display along with the original U.S. Constitution and the Bill of Rights. Together, these three historic documents are called the Charters of Freedom.

• The Declaration of Independence is sealed inside a special encasement made of titanium, aluminum, and bulletproof glass. The encasement contains argon gas, and the humidity inside it is carefully controlled to keep the parchment flexible.

• In the movie *National Treasure* (2004), characters looked for a clue to finding a secret treasure written in invisible ink on the back of the Declaration of Independence. The clue—and the treasure—are pure fiction, but there *is* writing on the flip side of the document. Years after the declaration was penned, a handwritten label was added. It reads, "Original Declaration of Independence, dated 4th July 1776."

Jefferson returned to the room he was renting and began to write. Braving the summer heat, he drew on all that he had read over the past thirty-three years of his life: theories from ancient philosophers, Enlightenment principles, the preamble to his draft of Virginia's constitution, and more. At his small desk, he recopied the document when it got too messy. He took short breaks to eat, to play his violin, and to buy gifts for his family. Some historians claim that Jefferson wrote the Declaration of Independence in a couple of days. Others say it took more than a week.

When he was done, Jefferson showed his work to Franklin and Adams, who made a few small edits. Originally, Jefferson wrote, "We hold these truths to be sacred and undeniable." Franklin changed it to read, "We hold these truths to be self-evident." Once the committee approved the document, Adams presented it to the Continental Congress. The delegates made major changes, such as deleting 630 words and adding 146. These revisions stung the thin-skinned Jefferson. "I was sitting by Dr. Franklin, who perceived that I was not insensible to these mutilations," he remembered.

In his draft, Jefferson took King George to task for the slave trade:

The Declaration of Independence Committee—Benjamin Franklin, John Adams, and Thomas Jefferson—review a draft of the Declaration of Independence.

He has waged cruel war against human nature itself, violating its most sacred rights of life and liberty in the persons of a distant people . . . captivating [taking them captive] and carrying them into slavery.

—Thomas Jefferson, original draft of
the Declaration of Independence

When delegates from the slave states of Georgia and South Carolina objected, Jefferson's section on slavery was cut.

Many people wonder how Jefferson, who owned six hundred slaves in his lifetime, could criticize Britain so harshly? As a young man, Jefferson made no secret of his dislike of slavery. He called it "an abominable crime" and a "moral depravity." He tried to get the slave trade outlawed in Virginia. Yet Jefferson also knew that plantations in the South, including Monticello, relied on slave labor to function. In 1776 there were close to half a million slaves living in the colonies. Slaves represented approximately 40 percent of Virginia's population at that time. Jefferson felt that to free the existing slaves would doom them to a life of unemployment and starvation, even as it doomed the South's economy. Jefferson blamed Britain for creating such an ugly, seemingly inescapable situation in the colonies.

On the Fourth of July, the Continental Congress adopted Jefferson's document. At the signing ceremony on August 2, Jefferson added his name to those of fifty-five other delegates at the bottom of the Declaration of Independence. It sealed his fate as a traitor to England and a founding father of the United States. Yet the fight for independence had just begun. Even as Jefferson was signing the declaration, 30,000 British soldiers were coming ashore on Staten Island, New York. The bloody Revolutionary

The Signing of the Declaration of Independence *was painted by the noted artist of the time, John Trumball.*

War continued until 1781, and it was not until 1783 that the king and Parliament officially recognized American independence.

The Declaration of Independence brought Jefferson no glory, for it was years before most Americans even knew who wrote it. Today, however, it is a priceless national treasure. Not all countries can recall the moment they came into being. But citizens of the United States know precisely where and when their country was born: in Philadelphia, Pennsylvania, on July 4, 1776.

LEADING VIRGINIA Three

With the Declaration of Independence finished, Thomas Jefferson was anxious to go home. He had been so tied up with the Second Continental Congress that he had had little time to grieve the death of his infant daughter, Jane. Also, childbirth had left Martha in frail health. Jefferson was desperate to get back to her.

Jefferson also missed serving in his home state. Virginia had recently adopted a constitution. Jefferson was eager to regain his legislative seat in the newly renamed Virginia House of Delegates. In September 1776 Jefferson was elected to the legislature's lower house. Over the next three years, he proposed 126 bills. Following are a few of the issues that Jefferson tackled.

UNIVERSAL EDUCATION

The Enlightenment taught Jefferson that the best governments are representative governments run by people who care about the common good and understand the issues that affect citizens' lives. Jefferson's bill for the More General Diffusion of Knowledge called for public schools in each county, and it guaranteed three years of education to all boys and girls. Under the law, a select group of promising boys would be chosen to move on to private school with all expenses paid. (Girls were not included because people believed they needed only enough education to prepare for marriage.) Jefferson thought the most talented students ought to have the best chance at an education "without regard to wealth, birth, or other accidental condition or circumstance."

Virginia had no public schools, so this was a radical idea. It was also an expensive one, which is why Jefferson's bill did not pass. Virginia would not set up a statewide public school system for another hundred years.

Religious Freedom

The Church of England, known as the Anglican Church, was the official church of Virginia. Regardless of their religion, colonists had to pay taxes to support the official church. Even

Colonial Virginians gather after church services. They were required to pay taxes to support the Church of England.

expressing opinions that contradicted church teachings could get you put to death in Virginia. Jefferson believed people should be free to worship as they pleased. He argued for a separation of church and state.

The legitimate powers of government extend to such acts only as are injurious to others. But it does me no injury for my neighbor to say there are twenty gods, or no God.

—Thomas Jefferson,
Notes on Virginia, 1784

JEFFERSON ON RELIGION

Thomas Jefferson viewed religion as a deeply personal matter. However, if pressed, he would call himself a Deist. Following the values of the Enlightenment, Deists believe that a supreme creator, or deity, created Earth and all its life forms. God exists, but is not actively involved in the daily events that unfold on the planet. Jefferson did attend church, but only because it was expected. He believed organized religion focused too much on the supernatural, rather than rational thought. He also thought religious leaders could be too harsh and judgmental. He once said, "My opinion is that there would have never been an infidel if there had never been a priest." Many other founding fathers and Enlightenment thinkers were Deists, including Benjamin Franklin, George Washington, Ethan Allen, and Thomas Paine.

In 1779 Jefferson's Virginia Act for Establishing Religious Freedom proclaimed that "no man shall be compelled to frequent or support any religious Worship place or Ministry whatsoever." The bill guaranteed people the freedom to express their own religious views. Much to Jefferson's frustration, the bill died—or so he thought. In time, others would take up Jefferson's torch for religious freedom with more success.

SLAVERY

In his book *Notes on Virginia*, Jefferson wrote that slavery "destroys the morals" of society by allowing "one half of the citizens thus to trample on the rights of the other." As a Virginia legislator, Jefferson proposed bills to allow slave owners to free their slaves or to end slavery. None passed. Giving liberty to slaves was not a popular idea among plantation owners, who

Slavery was a vital element to the livelihood of southern plantations in the colonies.

depended on slave labor to make a living. Jefferson tried other tactics, and in 1778 he led a successful fight to outlaw the importation of new slaves to Virginia.

Still, Jefferson's ideas and actions regarding slavery often contradicted each other. Back in 1769, his first year in the legislature, Jefferson asked senior lawmaker Richard Bland to propose a bill to make it legal for slave owners to free their slaves. This practice was known as **manumission**. It was a bold move. Bland proposed the bill and took some serious heat for it. Thirteen years later, Virginia finally enacted manumission laws. Thirty thousand African Americans got their freedom as many slaveholders released their slaves. Jefferson, however, was not one of them. Of the hundreds of slaves he owned, Jefferson freed only seven (two while he was alive and five more in his will). If Jefferson truly believed slavery was wrong, why didn't he free his slaves when it became legal to do so?

Jefferson likely defended his actions for several reasons. First, he knew that the agricultural South, as well as his own beloved Monticello, would collapse without slave labor. He treated his slaves better than most plantation owners. He paid overtime wages and allowed artisans to share in the profits of their work. He also believed that African Americans were inferior to whites and that freed slaves would be like children, ill equipped to fend for themselves in a white-dominated society. "Nothing would induce me to put my negroes out of my own protection," he wrote in 1820.

Still, how could a man who fought so hard for liberty, who penned "all men are created equal," who believed himself to be good and moral, participate in such an immoral practice? It was a question only Jefferson could answer, and he struggled with it his entire life. Jefferson saw slavery as a puzzle with no easy solution. By the mid-1780s, he gave up trying to pass legislation abolishing it. Jefferson left the issue for future generations to tackle.

But as it is, we have the wolf by the ears, and we can neither hold him, nor safely let him go. Justice is in one scale, and self-preservation in the other.

—Thomas Jefferson, 1820

State of Disaster

In June 1779 the Virginia legislature elected Jefferson to the first of two terms as governor. Jefferson knew it would be tough leading his state while the Revolutionary War was raging. What he did not fully realize was that his hands were tied. And he had helped supply the rope.

While under Britain's thumb, colonial lawmakers had seen the damage that a governor with too much control could do. Virginia's new constitution gave the state legislature supreme powers. Jefferson was happy to let the legislature make all decisions—that is, until he realized just how little power he had. Unlike today's governors, he could not **veto** a bill. Just to make routine budget decisions, Jefferson had to get the approval of an eight-man council. The war had plunged Virginia, and the entire union, into crisis. When the Continental Army begged Virginia to send money, weapons, and recruits, Jefferson did not have the authority to act quickly or to recruit effectively.

Once the wealthiest colony in America, Virginia was going through hard times. Britain was no longer importing Virginia tobacco. Inflation was out of control, and money was almost worthless. War costs were draining the state treasury. The bulk of the state's militia was fighting in the North and leaving Virginia almost defenseless. Fearing a sea invasion from British forces, legislators decided to move the capital inland, from Williamsburg to Richmond.

Jefferson was not a military strategist. He debated the morality of sending soldiers on missions without their approval. He found it difficult to give orders. When General George Washington, head of the Continental Army, sent word that the British planned to attack Virginia's new capital, Jefferson either waited too long or could not gather a militia. In January 1781 a British fleet sailed up the James River. It was led by General Benedict Arnold, an American traitor who had joined the British cause. Arnold's troops ransacked Richmond, setting buildings on fire and looting arms. Jefferson and other lawmakers fled the city. Jefferson pleaded with Washington for help, and the general sent 1,500 troops under the command of French major general Marquis de Lafayette. As the end of his second term approached, Jefferson knew he was "unprepared by his line of life and education for the command of armies." He announced that he would not seek reelection.

On May 31, 1781, Lord Charles Cornwallis, commander of British forces in Virginia, set out to capture Governor Jefferson and members of the Virginia legislature. A young militia captain named Jack Jouett saw the troops and guessed where they were headed. The twenty-six-year-old rode 40 miles in the middle of the night through the backwoods of Virginia to Monticello to warn Jefferson. The governor sent his family to safety at a neighbor's farm and stayed behind to gather some important papers. Another neighbor, Christopher Hudson, found Jefferson "perfectly tranquil and undisturbed" and told him to leave immediately. Jefferson did. British troops arrived at Monticello, found it empty, and drank their fill of Jefferson's wine before leaving.

While this crisis was happening, Jefferson's term as governor ended, even though the legislature had been unable to reconvene to elect a new governor. A private citizen once more, Jefferson rejoined his family and headed to Poplar Forest. Soon, rumors began flying that Jefferson had turned tail and run from the British. Worse, people were saying he had abandoned them by leaving the state without a governor.

Virginia lawmakers, led by George Nicholas and Patrick Henry, called for an investigation. On December 12, 1781, Jefferson arrived at the inquiry. Nicholas did not show up. Jefferson stood up and disproved the accusations against him. For someone uncomfortable with public speaking, this took great courage. Jefferson said that the legislature had known very well when he was leaving office, and he had spoken with various lawmakers about choosing General Thomas Nelson as his replacement. The charges against Jefferson were quickly dropped. The legislature then passed a resolution thanking Jefferson "for his impartial, upright, and attentive administration whilst in office." But the damage was done. Humiliated by the allegations, Jefferson announced he was through with public service:

I have taken my final leave of politics. I have retired to my farm, to my family and books, from which, I think, nothing will ever separate me.

—Thomas Jefferson, 1781

British commander General Charles Cornwallis, surrenders after the Battle of Yorktown.

The Revolutionary War was nearly over. Surrounded on all sides by French and American troops at Yorktown, Virginia, Cornwallis and his seven thousand troops surrendered. The Treaty of Paris, signed in 1783, made it official. The weary, war-torn former governor of Virginia was glad to be heading home. Yet even at Monticello, Jefferson found no peace.

A LOVE LOST

On May 20, 1782, Jefferson's wife, Martha, gave birth to their daughter, Lucy. The baby was fine, but Martha was gravely ill.

Circle of Friends

Imagine you are Thomas Jefferson, and colonial heavyweights like Benjamin Franklin, James Madison, and John Adams are your close friends. Jefferson deeply admired Franklin's intelligence, sense of humor, and scientific mind. The two shared political views, including a strong commitment to educating young people. Jefferson also found a kindred spirit in young Madison, a thoughtful, generally quiet Virginian. Madison's views mirrored those of Jefferson, his mentor, and the two men worked well together. Madison was one of the few people from whom Jefferson accepted constructive criticism.

At first glance, John Adams was the very opposite of Jefferson. A stout man, Adams was blunt, controversial, and a distinguised orator. He and Jefferson did not always agree on political matters, but they truly liked and respected each other. Jefferson once described Adams to Madison as "so amiable . . . I pronounce you will love him if you ever become acquainted with him."

Lucy was Martha's sixth child in ten years. Each birth had left her weaker than the last. Only two of Jefferson's six children, Patsy and Maria, lived beyond the age of three. For the next several months, Jefferson rarely left Martha's side.

It is said that on her deathbed, Martha asked Jefferson not to remarry. She had been raised by an unkind stepmother, and she did not want the same for her children. Whether the story is true or not, Jefferson never did remarry. On September 6, 1782, thirty-three-year-old Martha died. Jefferson sank into a deep depression. His wife's death "wiped away all my plans and left me a blank which I had not the spirits to fill up." For hours each day, Jefferson rode his horse through the Monticello countryside. Ten-year-old Patsy trailed behind her father to make sure he was all right:

> *And in those melancholy rambles I was his constant companion—a solitary witness to many a violent burst of grief.*
>
> —Patsy Jefferson

Friends such as James Madison and James Monroe reached out to Jefferson. The man who vowed never to return to public service soon discovered that politics was more than a career. It was his saving grace.

Path to the Presidency

*I*n spring 1783 Jefferson was back in the Continental Congress doing what he did best: writing legislation. Although Jefferson had never ventured any further west than the West Virginia border, the frontier intrigued him. In 1774 Jefferson proposed organizing the Northwest Territory, an area of more than 250,000 square miles. It covered present-day Ohio, Indiana, Illinois, Michigan, Wisconsin, and eastern Minnesota. He envisioned each area ruling itself under the guidance of the Continental Congress. As a territory grew in population, it could petition the congress to join the Union as a new state. Jefferson wanted to name the states, and he even came up with a list. Most of the American-Indian names did not make the cut, but Illonia did become Illinois and Michigania was shortened to Michigan.

Jefferson also wanted to outlaw slavery in the new states. Congress revised Jefferson's resolution over the course of several years' debate, and legislators agreed to ban slavery in the Northwest Ordinance of 1787, which carved out the boundaries for these new states. Jefferson's proposal for how to establish new states was eventually written into the U.S. Constitution.

American in Paris

In May 1784 Jefferson was on board a ship sailing across the Atlantic Ocean. After he arrived in Paris, the Continental Congress appointed him as the American minister to France, the colonies' Revolutionary War ally. A minister is a type of

Money Matters

Did you know that the monetary system we use today was Jefferson's idea? In the mid-1700s, the colonists used a hodgepodge of coins and bills from around the world—British pounds, Spanish dollars, German *ducats*, and Portuguese *moidores*, to name a few. Each colony had its own money and exchange rate. It was quite confusing. In 1784 Jefferson wrote a report, *Notes on the Establishment of a Money Unit*, suggesting that the Continental Congress use the simple decimal system for currency: one-cent, five-cent, ten-cent, twenty-five-cent, fifty-cent, and one-dollar units. The United States was the first country in the world to base a series of coins on the decimal system. Surprisingly, when Jefferson became president, he refused to allow his image to be used on any U.S. currency. He felt that stamping his face on a coin was too much like something Britain might do to pay tribute to royalty.

ambassador. Jefferson was to replace Benjamin Franklin, who had served in the role for six years. Franklin was almost eighty years old and ready to retire. Jefferson took his daughter Patsy and a slave named James Hemings with him to Paris. Maria came three years later, as well as James's fourteen-year-old sister, Sally. Sadly, Jefferson never saw his youngest daughter, Lucy, again. The two-year-old died of whooping cough only a few months after he set sail for France.

Jefferson enjoyed European art, music, and architecture. The people he met were kind and welcoming. Yet he also noticed

While in Europe, Thomas Jefferson enjoyed the upper-class culture of Paris.

disturbing divisions in society. The nobility and the wealthiest people controlled the government, hiked taxes, and flaunted their riches. It was a sharp contrast to the middle class and average working citizens, who suffered from high taxes, unemployment, and poverty. The situation only deepened Jefferson's belief that a government must belong to *all* its people:

If anybody thinks that kings, nobles, or priests are good conservators of the public happiness, send him here.

—Thomas Jefferson in a letter
to George Wythe, 1786

Jefferson had arrived in France at a critical time. The French Revolution was brewing. Before the century came to a close, King Louis XVI, Queen Marie Antoinette, and members of the French nobility would fall in a bloody revolt of the working class. Jefferson supported the right of the French people to change their government just as Americans had done. He hoped they would do it peacefully, but it was not to be. Strangely, the over-the-top displays of wealth Jefferson saw in Paris did not stop him from spending a ton of money trying to keep up with the lavish lifestyle. He bought the best food, wine, clothes, and furniture because it was expected of a distinguished diplomat. His love for reading made buying books a passion. All this spending sunk him into debt.

As the U.S. minister, Jefferson negotiated trade treaties with France, the Netherlands, Sweden, and other European countries. Now and then, he got the chance to work with his friend, John Adams, who was serving as a diplomat in London.

For Jefferson, letters from home were a precious treat. Each one took up to two months to cross the Atlantic. Some of the news was quite extraordinary. In 1786 James Madison wrote that Patrick Henry had proposed a bill in the Virginia legislature to use taxes to pay the salaries of religious leaders. In response, Madison had revived Jefferson's Bill for Religious Freedom, and the bill had passed. Jefferson was thrilled. Later, Jefferson looked upon this as one of his greatest political achievements.

This portrait of Thomas Jefferson was painted by Mather Brown around the time Jefferson was U.S. minister to France.

MATTERS OF THE HEART

While in Paris, Jefferson fell for a blue-eyed portrait painter named Maria Cosway. Born in Italy to English parents, Maria was young, beautiful, and charming. She was also married (though unhappily). In 1786 the forty-three-year-old widower and the twenty-seven-year-old artist spent a whirlwind summer together touring art galleries, museums, and

monuments. Once, while strolling with Maria, Jefferson showed off by jumping over a low fence. He fell and dislocated his wrist. The injury was not set properly, and the wrist never healed correctly. That fall, when Maria left Paris with her husband, Jefferson wrote her a twelve-page letter—certainly a difficult task given his painfed wrist. In the letter, the characters Head and Heart—meaning reason and emotion—debate their delicate situation:

Head. Well, friend, you seem to be in a pretty trim.
Heart. I am indeed the most wretched of all earthly beings.
Head. This is one of the scrapes into which you are ever leading us.
Heart. Oh, my friend! this is no moment to upbraid my foibles. I am
rent into fragments by the force of my grief!

—Thomas Jefferson, letter to
Maria Cosway, October 12, 1786

Though his heart longed to be with Maria, Jefferson's head knew it was impossible. There could be no future for them together. The couple went their separate ways. However, they remained friends and occasionally wrote to each other.

Jefferson also heard about a massive uprising by citizens in Massachusetts. Faced with high taxes, imprisonment, and loss of land to inflexible creditors, a group of poor farmers had begun storming the state courts. Led by Daniel Shays, a former captain in the Continental Army, they had even busted in on the state supreme court in Springfield. The revolt grew until it involved nearly one-quarter of New England's farmers. Shays's Rebellion, as it came to be known, was finally squelched by a Massachusetts militia of four thousand soldiers. Jefferson applauded the uprising. "I hold it, that a little rebellion, now and then, is a good thing, and as necessary in the political world as storms in the physical," he wrote Madison.

Shays's Rebellion brought home the point that the young country needed a strong national constitution spelling out the powers of the government and the rights of individuals. Since 1781 the United States had been operating under the Articles of Confederation, a loosely knit union of independent states. There was no president. No federal court system. No strong central government.

In the winter of 1787 James Madison sent Jefferson a draft of the proposed U.S. Constitution. Jefferson replied that he liked the document, but he thought it should have a bill of rights clearly defining the rights of citizens, such as "freedom of religion, freedom of the press, protection against standing armies, restriction of monopolies . . . and trials by jury." Madison agreed to argue for a bill of rights in the Constitution. It was a tough fight against outspoken opponents like Patrick Henry and George Clinton (New York). In 1791 the first ten amendments, which make up the Bill of Rights, were added to the U.S. Constitution.

In September 1789 Jefferson received permission to travel to the United States from France for a visit. He packed up more than thirty boxes of books, along with European delicacies including macaroni, raisins, and Parmesan cheese. Jefferson planned to spend six months at

Daniel Shays led a revolt in 1787 in response to imposed taxes and other threats to the colonists.

Thomas Jefferson is welcomed home from Paris by his slaves in 1789.

Monticello before returning to France. However, the United States had just elected its first president, and George Washington had other plans for Thomas Jefferson.

RED, WHITE, AND BLUE POLITICS

Jefferson had barely set foot on Virginia soil when he received a letter from the president. Washington wanted Jefferson to be part of his new cabinet. A cabinet is a group of experts who advise the president on matters like war, money, the law, and foreign policy. With the urging of James Madison, Washington had appointed Jefferson as the nation's first secretary of state. Jefferson was to be the president's chief advisor. He was third in line for the presidency after his friend, John Adams, who had been elected vice president. Before heading to New York, the nation's temporary capital, Jefferson went home to Monticello to arrange Patsy's wedding.

Jefferson's job was to lead the cabinet, which consisted of Henry Knox as secretary of war, Alexander Hamilton as secretary of treasury, and Edmund Randolph in the position of attorney general. At first, Jefferson worked well with the other cabinet members. But soon it became obvious that the secretary of state and the secretary of treasury did not see eye to eye on economics, government, world affairs, or pretty much anything.

Alexander Hamilton, more than a decade younger than Jefferson, was one of Washington's most trusted officers in the Continental Army. The thirty-four-year-old attorney from New York was bright and bold. Hamilton did not share Jefferson's Enlightenment value that people were basically good. He did not trust ordinary citizens to run the government. "The people!" he once cried. "The people is a great beast!"

Hamilton favored the British style of government, in which royalty and the upper classes ruled. He thought a small group of elite businessmen ought to run the U.S government. In his view, the nation needed a powerful central government with an emphasis on business and industry, not agriculture. Jefferson, by contrast, envisioned a nation of farmers. He believed the government should be accessible and accountable to the people. That could only be

Alexander Hamilton favored the British style of government and often opposed the views of Thomas Jefferson.

accomplished if the states held the balance of power. Jefferson felt Hamilton's view of a ruling aristocracy of the wealthy betrayed everything America had fought for in the Revolution:

Hamilton was . . . so bewitched and perverted by the British example, as to be under thorough conviction that corruption was essential to the government of a nation.

—Thomas Jefferson, 1818

Jefferson and Hamilton clashed again over the establishment of a national bank. Hamilton favored it. Jefferson worried that such a bank would increase government power, enlarge the debt, and encourage corruption. Using a strict interpretation of the Constitution, he argued that the document did not give Congress the right to establish a bank. Hamilton shot back that the Constitution did not say Congress did *not* have the right. In his loose interpretation of the Constitution, Hamilton referred to the section that gave government the right "to make all laws which shall be necessary and proper." Hamilton got his bank. Jefferson got annoyed that his political enemy had more influence over the president than he did.

The differences between Washington's two top advisors split the administration into two camps. Those who supported Hamilton, such as John Adams, were known as Federalists. Politicians who sided with Jefferson, such as James Madison and Edmund Randolph, were called Antifederalists, or Republicans (the name was later changed to Democratic-Republicans, then Democrats). The ongoing battles between Jefferson and Hamilton took a toll on President Washington, who valued both of his cabinet officers:

My earnest wish, and my fondest hope therefore is, that instead of wounding suspicions, and irritable charges, there may be liberal allowances—mutual forbearances—and temporizing yielding on all sides.

—George Washington, in a letter to
Thomas Jefferson, August 1792

Despite his president's plea, Jefferson was not ready to shake hands. He believed the Federalists were bent on destroying his reputation and career. Hamilton felt the Republicans were doing the same to him.

In 1793 Britain and France were once again at war. Hamilton's Federalists supported Britain. Jefferson's Republicans backed France, now under the control of revolutionary forces after King Louis's execution. The two top U.S. advisors found one point to agree on: the United States should stay out of the conflict, if possible.

France's new U.S. ambassador, Edmond Charles Édouard Genêt, was trying every political trick he knew to draw the United States into the war. Genêt's threats to appeal directly to the American people infuriated Jefferson. A diplomat was not supposed to behave that way in a foreign country. After more than three years of wrangling with Hamilton, the Federalists, and the French, Jefferson was ready to call it quits. At the close of Washington's first term, Jefferson turned in his resignation. Swearing off politics for good, Jefferson headed to Monticello. Again.

SECOND IN COMMAND

At home, Thomas Jefferson got to work restoring his long-neglected plantation. To earn additional money, he set up a

A Scientific Mind

Ever the scientist, Jefferson was always tinkering with some new innovation to improve life or to solve a problem. Here are a few of his most notable innovations:

- Wheel cipher—while serving as secretary of state, Jefferson devised an encryption device that used a set of spinning wheels to scramble and unscramble secret messages.

- Moldboard—Jefferson came up with a new design for the part of a plow that lifts and turns dirt. His invention made it easier and more efficient for a plow to move through the soil.

- The great clock—powered by two sets of cannonball-like weights, Jefferson's windup clock gave both the time and the day of the week.

- Polygraph—this machine was used for copying. The wooden frame held two pens above two pieces of paper. As Jefferson wrote on one page, the other pen copied the text onto a separate page exactly as he had written it.

Jefferson's other clever inventions included a revolving bookstand that held five books, a globe-shaped sundial, a concave mirror, a swivel chair, and a solar microscope.

nail-making area in his blacksmith shop. It was quite a profitable business. In the late 1790s slaves working at Jefferson's nailery turned out between five thousand and ten thousand nails a day. Hoping to lure him back into politics, Jefferson's friends kept him up to date on current events. Secretly, Jefferson was itching to get back into the game. He was about to get his chance.

On September 19, 1796, Washington published his farewell address in the *Pennsylvania Packet* newspaper. He would not seek a third term. Now, with two distinct political parties locked in battle, it was clear the election of 1796 was going to be interesting. A newspaper editor wrote,

> *It requires no talent at divination to decide who will be candidates for the chair. THOMAS JEFFERSON & JOHN ADAMS will be the men, & whether we shall have at the head of our executive a steadfast friend of the Rights of the People, or an advocate for hereditary power and distinctions, the people of the United States are soon to decide.*

> —The Philadelphia *Aurora*, 1796

The Republicans never asked Jefferson if he wanted to be president. They simply put him on the ballot with Aaron Burr, a senator from New York, as his running mate. But Jefferson was willing to stand for office because he feared what the Federalists might do to subvert the Constitution. The Federalists put up Jefferson's old friend, John Adams and Thomas Pinckney of South Carolina. Federalists took pot shots at Jefferson. They called him a coward. They exaggerated the incident at the end of Jefferson's governorship, when Virginia was left without a governor during the Revolutionary War. They accused him of being an atheist and tagged him as an extremist supporter of the rebel French government. The Republicans fired back, claiming Adams was a monarchist—a lover of the British royal system—and un-American.

In the late 1700s there was no election day when people voted for the candidates. Instead, the president and vice president were chosen by the electoral college, a group of legislators. Every state chose its own electors, either by popular vote or in the state legislature. Each elector voted for two candidates, and the ballots were sent to the nation's capitol to be counted. The candidate with the most votes was named president, and the runner-up got to be vice president.

In the election of 1796, when the electoral votes were counted, John Adams squeaked past his old friend, Jefferson, seventy-one to sixty-eight. Thomas Pinckney got fifty-nine votes, and Aaron Burr received thirty. That was okay with Jefferson, who claimed to prefer coming in second or third so he could spend more time at Monticello.

Although Adams was not a fanatical Federalist like Hamilton, it did not take long for party politics to create tension between the newly elected president and his vice president. Their differing views on the war between Britain and France continued to separate them. Almost from inauguration day, relations were rocky. Jefferson said Adams never came to him for advice on governmental matters. Newspapers fanned the flames of discontent. Their once-close friendship soon soured.

Vice President Jefferson saw his main task as presiding over the Senate—a job for which he was well suited. He loved the ins and outs of legislative rules. In 1800 he published *A Manual of Parliamentary Practice*, in which he clarified how to conduct

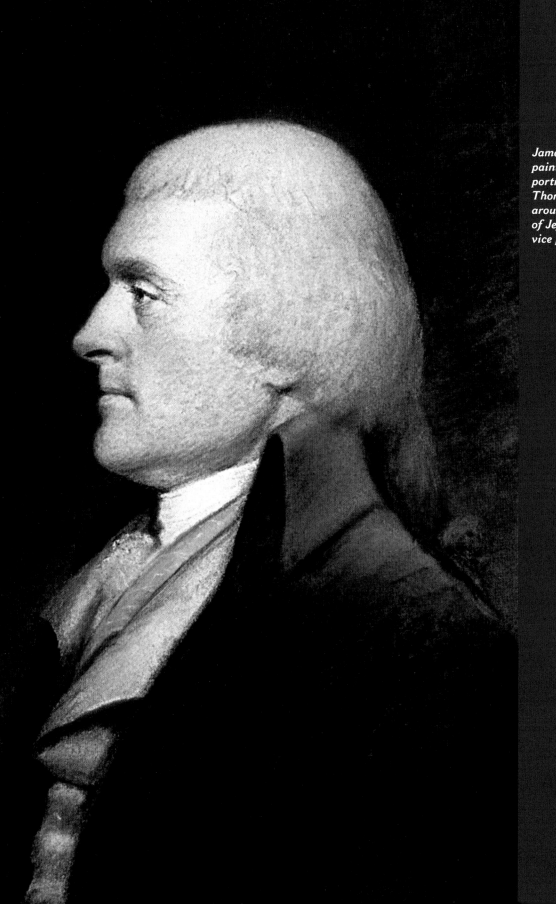

James Sharple painted this portrait of Thomas Jefferson around the time of Jefferson's vice presidency.

legislative business. The manual is still in print today, and the representatives still refer to it for questions about procedure.

Angry about the Americans' neutral stance in the war, France began seizing American merchant ships and cargo. U.S. diplomats tried to talk to the new French government, called The Directory, but were repeatedly turned away. Adams did not want to be drawn into war, but he knew it was a possibility. He created the U.S. Department of Navy to build up American defenses in case peace negotiations failed.

In the meantime, the Federalist-controlled Congress passed the Alien and Sedition Acts. The laws made it illegal for anyone to speak out against the president or the government. Jefferson was outraged. This was a blatant attempt to squelch Republican newspapers, as well as the free speech of all Americans. James Madison agreed. The pair wrote a set of resolutions stating that the acts were unconstitutional. They became known as the Kentucky and Virginia Resolutions, after the states in which they were introduced and passed. Much to Jefferson's disappointment, no other states adopted the resolutions. The Alien and Sedition Acts eventually expired.

Jefferson had long felt the Federalists posed a threat to American liberties. The Sedition Acts had proven it. He quietly took the reins of the Republican Party to lead it into the new century. As Adams's first term in office wound down, Jefferson was no longer content to be second in command. He wanted to lead. He wanted to be president.

THE PEOPLE'S PRESIDENT

Five

$\mathcal{O}$n the morning of March 4, 1801, fifty-seven-year-old Thomas Jefferson stepped out of his boarding house in Washington, D.C. Surrounded by a small group of friends and well-wishers, he began walking toward the capitol. The nation's capital had recently been relocated from Philadelphia, and much of Washington was still under construction—including the President's House and the capitol. Jefferson would be the first U.S. president to take his oath of office in the new capitol.

For their inaugurations, Washington and Adams had dressed in their finest clothes and had worn swords. Not the third president. "His dress was, as usual, that of a plain citizen, without any distinctive badge of office," said a reporter. There was no marching band, no grand parade, no elegant carriage ride. In the Senate chamber before a standing-room-only crowd, Chief Justice John Marshall swore Jefferson into office. Bitter after losing a tough election, outgoing president John Adams did not attend the ceremony. He was not there to hear the man he had once called a friend say the following:

> *Let us, then, fellow-citizens, unite with one heart and one mind. Let us restore to social intercourse that harmony and affection without which liberty and even life itself are but dreary things . . . every difference of opinion is not a difference of principle. We have called by*

Thomas Jefferson was known for his less than elegant dress, even at his own inauguration.

different names brethren of the same principle. We are all republicans—we are federalists.

—Thomas Jefferson, inaugural
address, March 4, 1801

Jefferson hoped his words would bring peace between the parties. It had been a long, grueling election process. In early 1800 the Republicans had again nominated Jefferson for president, with Burr as his running mate. The Federalists were backing President Adams and Pinckney. The campaign was brutal, and both sides hurled ugly accusations at each other. At one point, to keep people from voting, the Federalists spread a rumor that Jefferson was dead.

It took seven months for the electoral votes to come trickling in from all sixteen states. When they did, the result was shocking. President Adams had come in third, with sixty-five electoral votes. Jefferson and Burr had tied for the presidency with seventy-three votes each. How could this happen? Everyone knew Jefferson was running for president, with Burr as vice president. However, on the ballot, electors were asked only to vote for two candidates, without specifying the office.

The U.S. Constitution required that the House of Representatives end the deadlock. Each state got one vote, and to win, a candidate needed a majority. The tricky part was that the majority in Congress were Federalists. These representatives were not thrilled about having to choose a president, as they saw it, "among Rotten Apples." Some Republicans were angry at Burr for not making a public statement and politely stepping aside. Finally, after a week of fierce debate and thirty-six separate votes, Jefferson won the presidency.

This presidential campaign poster from 1800 declares "Thomas Jefferson, President of the U.S.A. / John Adams, no more."

Amazingly, it was Jefferson's old foe, Alexander Hamilton, who boosted him to victory. Hamilton did not like Jefferson, but he loathed Burr, who had defeated Hamilton's brother-in-law to become a U.S. senator. Hamilton accused Burr of being selfish and "bankrupt beyond redemption." Hamilton persuaded many Federalist lawmakers to put Jefferson over the top instead of Burr (Burr became vice president). To prevent a similar election crisis from happening again, Congress added the Twelfth Amendment

Your Humble Servant

Visitors to the President's House were often surprised to be greeted by President Jefferson dressed in casual clothes and slippers. In keeping with his view that the presidency should not become a monarchy, Jefferson liked to keep things simple and informal. Gone were the fancy receptions and dinners that Washington and Adams had hosted. Jefferson wrote all of his own speeches, letters, and state papers on stationery that had no presidential seal. He did not accept gifts for fear of impropriety. Once, when a Massachusetts ministry presented him with a 1,200-pound wheel of cheese, Jefferson paid two hundred dollars for it, and then spent the next several years trying to give it away!

Concerned that the State of the Union address too closely mimicked the ceremonies of Parliament, Jefferson chose not to speak directly to Congress (his shyness may also have factored into this decision). In December 1801, Jefferson had his aide, Meriwether Lewis, deliver his first State of the Union message at the capitol and read it out loud to Congress. It was the beginning of a presidential tradition that lasted for more than a hundred years.

to the Constitution in 1804. It required electors to declare a choice for president and vice president on their ballots.

The election of 1800 proved to be historical in another way. It marked the first time a republic had peacefully transferred power from one party to another. There was no violence or bloodshed, as often occurred when governments changed hands in Europe. Years later Jefferson called it "the revolution of 1800," saying it "was as real a revolution in the principles of our government as that of 1776 was in its form; not effected indeed by the sword, as that, but by the rational and peaceful instrument of reform, the suffrage of the people."

CHANGING COURSE

By inauguration day, U.S peace talks with France had proven successful. With the threat of war gone, Jefferson turned his attention to selecting a cabinet. He named Albert Gallatin, treasurer of the Republican Party, as secretary of treasury. James Madison was chosen as secretary of state. Henry Dearborn, a Massachusetts congressman and a Revolutionary War hero, was appointed secretary of war. The new president had two main political goals: first, to establish a strong partnership within his cabinet, and second, to create an atmosphere of cooperation with Republican leaders in Congress.

True to his ideals of small government, Jefferson was determined to cut what he considered irresponsible Federalist spending. Jefferson instructed Gallatin to reduce the national debt by 30 percent, while putting in place a plan to pay off the entire national debt in sixteen years. Jefferson slashed the budgets of the military and reduced the size of the standing army and navy. He repealed all internal taxes, including a business tax on whiskey that was unpopular in the West. He even did away with the Internal Revenue Service.

Initially, Jefferson spent much of this time replacing Federalist government officials with Republicans. In the final weeks of John Adams's presidency, when it became clear he was not going to win reelection, Adams had raced to fill the courts

PIRATES OF THE MEDITERRANEAN

Since the early 1500s, merchant ships in the Mediterranean Sea off the northern coast of Africa were at risk of attack from pirates. Sailing from Algiers, Tripoli, Tunisia, and Morocco, the Barbary pirates seized ships and held the crew and cargo for ransom. Many European nations, as well as the United States, paid bribe money called tribute to the leaders of these states to keep the pirates at bay.

(continued)

Since his days as minister to France, Jefferson had strongly disapproved of this practice. As minister, he had tried, and failed, to get Europe to join the United States in stopping the payoffs by force. In 1801 the pasha, or ruler, of Tripoli began targeting American ships for attack. He demanded an increase in tribute. Jefferson was not about to budge. He sent four warships to the Mediterranean. The pasha declared war on the United States. For four years, the United States and Tripoli waged small naval battles in the Mediterranean until the pasha finally agreed to peace. The tribute payments stopped, but the Barbary pirate attacks continued in the region for more than a decade.

with Federalists judges. Jefferson condemned these last-minute appointments, many done under the quickly passed Judiciary Act of 1801. Jefferson could not remove many of the judges, but he could stop Madison from delivering the official paperwork to those who had yet to take office. William Marbury and three other Adams appointees were not amused. They asked the Supreme Court to order Madison to turn over the commissions. In *Marbury vs. Madison*, Chief Justice Marshall, a Federalist, ruled that while Marbury was entitled to his commission, the court could not force Madison to give it to him. Why? The law giving the court authority was unconstitutional. This ruling paved the way for the doctrine of judicial review, which gave the Supreme Court power to declare acts of Congress unconstitutional.

What a Deal!

Not long after Jefferson took office, he heard rumblings that Spain was planning to **cede** the Louisiana Territory to its original owner, France. The territory was a huge chunk of land, covering 827,000 square miles of the American West. It stretched south from the Canadian border to the Gulf of Mexico, and east from the Mississippi River to the Rocky Mountains. If the rumors were true, France would soon control the port city of New Orleans and the Mississippi River, a key American trading route. France firmly denied the report, but Jefferson stayed on his toes.

In fall 1802 Spain officially turned over the Louisiana Territory to France. Jefferson sent the U.S. minister to France, Robert Livingston, to try to convince French leader Napoleon Bonaparte to sell New Orleans to the United States. However, Napoleon and his foreign minister, Charles Maurice de Talleyrand, refused to see Livingston. In early 1803 Jefferson tried again. This time he sent James Monroe, whom he had trained as a lawyer and who had been his aide when he was governor of Virginia. Monroe was told to offer Napoleon $10 million for New Orleans and the Floridas or, at the very least, do what he could to acquire access to the port and the Mississippi River.

Before Monroe could even arrive in France, Talleyrand made Livingston a surprising proposal. France wanted to do more than sell New Orleans to the United States. It wanted to sell the entire Louisiana Territory! The asking price was $15 million (about three cents per acre). After years of warfare, and with another clash with Britain looming, France needed the money. When Monroe set foot on French soil, the two American ministers sealed the

James Monroe and Robert Livingston discuss the Louisiana Purchase with France's Minister Talleyrand.

deal. The treaty was signed in early May. When Jefferson heard the news he was amazed and delighted:

> *The territory acquired, as it includes all the waters of the Missouri and Mississippi, has more than doubled the area of the United States, and the new parts is not inferior to the old in soil, climate, productions, and important communications.*

> —Thomas Jefferson, letter to General Horatio Gates, July 11, 1803

Touched by Scandal

In 1802 James T. Callender, a journalist who had once helped Jefferson take some stinging shots at the Federalists, turned his sights on the president. As editor of the *Richmond Recorder* newspaper, Callender wrote an article claiming Jefferson had fathered a child with a slave. "Her name is Sally," he claimed. Callender was referring to Sally Hemings, the slave who had accompanied Jefferson's daughter, Maria, to Paris. Sally was believed to be the daughter of Betty Hemings and John Wayles, which made her a half sister to Jefferson's deceased wife, Martha.

Spread by Federalists, the story haunted Jefferson throughout his presidency and beyond. But was it true? We cannot know for sure, because neither Jefferson nor Sally Hemings ever spoke or wrote about the matter. We do know that years after Jefferson's death, two of Sally's six children, Eston and Madison, told people that their mother had informed them that Jefferson was their father. Historians still debate the results of DNA tests done on Jefferson's male descendents in the late 1990s. The results indicated that a male in the Jefferson family was likely Eston's father. But no one can be certain if it was Jefferson or another family member. Interestingly, Jefferson, who rarely freed any of his slaves, gave all of Sally Hemings's children their freedom. He freed two of her children in the final years of his life, and two more in his will. Was this move an indication of his involvement with Sally? Many historians are convinced that it was.

Jefferson was also worried, however. There was nothing in the U.S. Constitution giving the federal government power to purchase land. What if the treaty was illegal? A strict interpreter of the Constitution, Jefferson began drafting a new amendment. Getting it passed, however, was going to take time—time the United States did not have. Monroe was reporting that Napoleon was thinking about backing out of the deal. Jefferson needed to act quickly. And he did. He went straight to Congress for approval of the funds. He got it, though only one Federalist voted in favor. Most politicians and citizens applauded the Louisiana Purchase, but many Federalists criticized Jefferson for changing his views on strict interpretation of the constitution when it suited him.

Jefferson was, at last, finding his political footing. He was becoming more confident and decisive as a leader. On December 20, 1803, the Louisiana Territory officially became part of the United States. The mystery and promise of the American West beckoned. Thomas Jefferson did not waste a minute.

NEW HORIZONS

*N*early fifty years had passed since a Virginia mapmaker and his young son had dreamed of what lay beyond their home in the Blue Ridge Mountains. Now, as president of the United States, Thomas Jefferson was ready to find out.

In 1801 more than 5 million people lived in the United States—two-thirds of them within 50 miles of the Atlantic Ocean. The Mississippi River was the edge of the western frontier. In his inaugural address, Jefferson shared his vision of "a rising nation, spread over a wise and fruitful land, traversing all the seas . . . advancing rapidly to destinies beyond the reach of mortal eye." Soon after his speech, Jefferson began outlining a plan for his country's first overland expedition of the American West. One of his goals was to find the Northwest Passage, a water route connecting the Pacific and Atlantic oceans. For centuries European explorers had tried and failed to find this mythical waterway. Jefferson wanted to know if it existed. He also wanted to know more about American-Indian cultures, plants, animals, geography, and climate in the region.

In February 1803 Congress approved $2,500 to fund the expedition, called the Corps of Discovery (the cost eventually soared to nearly $40,000). That spring Jefferson asked twenty-eight-year-old Meriwether Lewis (1744–1809) to lead the exploration party. An army captain and naturalist, Lewis had been Jefferson's personal aide. Jefferson considered him "brave, prudent, habituated to the woods and familiar with

In 1801, around the time this portrait was painted, Thomas Jefferson had a vision of exploration and expansion of the American West.

LOST CIVILIZATION

Jefferson was eager to learn as much as he could about American-Indian traditions, laws, languages, and lifestyle. Yet while he was fascinated with native culture, he was also instrumental in destroying it. Jefferson felt American Indians were "in body and mind equal to the white man," but they needed to blend in to western society. He believed tribes should settle on farms as the Europeans had, even though many American Indians already lived in villages. Such settlement would, of course, free up hunting grounds for white expansion.

(continued)

Through this "civilization program," American Indians were not supposed to be forced to sell or to give up their lands, but pressure was often applied in other ways. Jefferson wrote a letter to future president William Henry Harrison, who was in charge of Indian affairs in the Indiana Territory. Jefferson suggested that American Indians be encouraged to buy goods on credit. Indians who fell into debt might then be persuaded to settle up by handing their land over to the government. During Jefferson's presidency, the United States bought more than 50 million acres of tribal lands for a total cost of under $150,000. It was only the beginning. The Louisiana Territory gave the United States a place to "remove" tribes east of Mississippi when they chose not to cooperate. In years to come, American-Indian leaders such as Shawnee chief Tecumseh led their tribes in fighting back against this land grabbing. They had little success. In time, the bloody conflicts, forced removals, and European diseases nearly destroyed the American-Indian way of life. A few years before his death, Jefferson acknowledged the treatment of American Indians as a "blot in our moral history," surpassed only by slavery.

Indian manners and character." Lewis asked a friend from his army days, Lieutenant William Clark (1770–1838), to be co-commander. Jefferson gave Lewis a long list of instructions about what he wanted the team to do—everything from noting the temperature of mineral water to making first contact with American-Indian nations:

*In all your intercourse with the natives treat them in the most friendly
and conciliatory manner which their own conduct will admit.*

—Thomas Jefferson, Instructions to
Meriwether Lewis, June 20, 1803

On May 21, 1804, the forty-eight-member Corps of Discovery set out from St. Louis and traveled up the Missouri River. The expedition was gone for almost two and a half years. Upon their return Jefferson was filled with "unspeakable joy," for he had given them up for lost. Lewis and Clark had not found the Northwest Passage, but the president and the nation could hardly be disappointed. In its 8,000-mile trek, the Corps of Discovery had made contact with numerous American-Indian tribes, discovered

Captain Meriwether Lewis and William Clark encounter American Indians on their expedition of the West.

hundreds of new plant and animal species, and mapped the journey over the Rocky Mountains and up the Columbia River to the Pacific Ocean.

The year 1804 was bittersweet for Thomas Jefferson. That spring, his twenty-five-year-old daughter, Maria Jefferson Eppes, died. Like her mother, she had always been in frail health. And like her mother, she died a few months after giving birth. Drowning in grief, Jefferson wrote to his old friend John Page that "I . . . have lost even the half of what I had. My evening prospects now hang on the slender thread of a single life." He was referring to Patsy. Of Jefferson's six children, only she remained.

Among most Americans, Jefferson was a popular president. He received hundreds of letters each week at the President's House, and most were positive. Printers raced to keep up with the public's demand for images of the third president. Although Jefferson had not originally planned on serving two terms, he agreed to do so now.

A ROCKY TERM

Some Republican Party members thought Aaron Burr had not done enough to secure Jefferson's election in 1801, when the two men were tied in electoral votes. Also wary of Burr, Jefferson had not made him part of the inner circle during his first term. In 1804 Burr was dropped as Jefferson's running mate in favor of New York governor George Clinton. The Federalists nominated Charles Pinckney for president and Rufus King of New York for vice president. The election of 1804 was very different from the heated, neck-and-neck race of 1800.

This time Jefferson won by a landslide, taking fourteen of sixteen states. Although he did not announce it, Jefferson knew

Thomas Jefferson's popularity sparked a big demand for images of the third president, printers could barely keep up.

THE BURR CONSPIRACY

After being tossed from the Republican presidential ticket in 1804, Aaron Burr ran for governor of New York. Once again, the outspoken Alexander Hamilton made no secret of his contempt for Burr. Burr lost the election. Furious that Hamilton's jabs had cost him the governor's race, Burr and Hamilton clashed again. Their argument ended when Burr challenged his old foe to a duel. Hamilton was seriously wounded in the duel, and died the next day.

To avoid arrest, Burr fled the East Coast in disgrace and headed west. He sought to invest in land in the Louisiana Territory, but some people believed he was plotting to separate the region from the United States and form an alliance with Spain. "We have traitors among us," Kentucky district attorney Joseph Daveiss (a Federalist) wrote to Jefferson. "A separation of the union in favour of Spain, is the object." The plot became known as the Burr Conspiracy. Jefferson had his former vice president arrested and tried for treason. "Yet although there is not a man in the United States who is not satisfied of the depth of his guilt, such are the jealous provisions of our laws in favor of the accused, and against the accuser, that I question if he can be convicted," wrote Jefferson. He was right. At the trial, Chief Justice Marshall tossed out most of the flimsy evidence and defined treason in such a way that Burr walked away a free man. Burr's political career, however, was finished.

this was to be his final term. Like George Washington before him, he had no wish to serve more than eight years in office. Jefferson had little time to celebrate his easy victory. The most difficult crisis of his presidency was about to unfold.

France and Britain were at war again. Napoleon had blockaded Britain to cut off sea trade, while Britain was forbidding other European countries from trading with France. Both sides were deliberately trying to drag the United States into war. Often, they captured American ships that they claimed were sailing for the other side. The British boarded American vessels and took away sailors they insisted had **deserted** the Royal Navy. Sometimes this was true, but most of the time it was not (only about one in ten sailors was a British deserter). The Royal Navy was in desperate need of sailors and often took whomever they could capture. Jefferson was horrified by these **impressments**, but he knew he had to be careful if he wanted to avoid getting caught up in the war.

In 1807 the Royal Navy alerted its ships along the U.S. coastline that the American frigate *Chesapeake* was harboring British deserters. On June 22 the captain of the British ship *Leopard* spotted the *Chesapeake*. He ordered Captain James Barron to turn over the men. When Barron said he had no deserters onboard, the *Leopard* fired its guns. Three of the *Chesapeake*'s sailors were killed, and eighteen more were injured. The British captured four men, though only one was found to be a deserter.

Americans were outraged. So was Jefferson. "This country has never been in such a state of excitement since the battle of Lexington," he said. Tensions mounted as the British threatened more impressments. France announced its intention to blockade U.S. ships, too. Something had to be done. Many Americans called for war. Jefferson was against it. He preferred an **embargo**. Secretary of State Madison agreed. Together, they pressed Congress to enact the Embargo Act of 1807. It kept all American ships from sailing to European ports. Jefferson figured France and Britain would soon buckle under the pressure because both heavily relied on American goods. However, he did not fully calculate how much America relied on Britain and France, too.

The British navy impresses seamen after the defeat of USS Chesapeake *by HMS* Leopard *in 1807.*

With U.S. ships virtually dead in the water, American merchants, fishermen, farmers, craftsman, and shippers suffered huge losses. In two years, the nation's income dropped from $16 million to less than $7 million. Businesses and farms failed.

Unemployment soared. Americans were upset, and they let their president know it. New England's fishing industry was hit particularly hard, which sparked this cutting Federalist rhyme:

Our ships all in motion once whitened the ocean,
They sailed and returned with a cargo;
Now all laid away, they fall into decay,
To Jefferson, worms, and EMBARGO.

Many members of Jefferson's own cabinet, including Secretary of Treasury Gallatin, opposed the embargo. True, it had kept the United States out of war. (Ultimately, the United States and Britain did clash in the War of 1812.) But at what cost? The U.S. economy was suffering far more than that of either France or Britain. After more than a year, it became clear Jefferson's strategy was not working. Congress waited for direction from Jefferson to repeal the embargo, but he hesitated. His term was nearly over, and he felt the decision should be made by the next president, James Madison. In the presidential election of 1808, Madison had easily defeated Charles Pinckney. Finally, in early 1809, Congress took steps to repeal the Embargo Act. Just three days before the end of his term, Jefferson signed it into law. It was his final major act as president of the United States.

Within a few days I retire to my family, my books, and farms. . . .
Never did a prisoner, released from his chains, feel such relief as I
shall on shaking off the shackles of power.

—Thomas Jefferson to Pierre Samuel
Du Pont de Nemours, March 2, 1809

On March 4, 1809, Jefferson rode up Pennsylvania Avenue to the capitol with his grandson. He joined the crowd in the House of Representatives to watch Madison become the fourth president of the United States. Albert Gallatin's young niece, Frances Few, recalled that "Mr. Jefferson appeared one of the most happy among this concourse of people." And why not? After forty years of public service, Thomas Jefferson felt he had fulfilled his duty to the nation. He was, truly and finally, going home.

Upon his retirement from the presidency, Thomas Jefferson returned to his beloved Virginia home, Monticello.

THE PURSUIT OF HAPPINESS

*O*nly family meant more to Thomas Jefferson than his mountaintop home in Virginia. Upon his return, the sixty-five-year-old had plenty of work ahead of him: repairing buildings and equipment, running the nailery, and tending crops. He also wanted to make up for lost time with Patsy and his grandchildren. It was heaven.

My mornings are devoted to correspondence. From breakfast to dinner I am in my shops, my garden, or on horseback among my farms; from dinner to dark, I give to society and recreation with my neighbors and friends; and from candle light to early bed-time I read.

—Thomas Jefferson to General
Thaddeus Kosciusko, February 26, 1810

Life was not completely carefree. Jefferson had gotten even deeper into financial trouble while president. He planned on selling some of his lands and possessions to pay off the debts and to finance his retirement. One thing he had not planned on giving up was his vast collection of books. Jefferson wanted the Library of Congress to get the first crack at buying his personal library after his death. But the War of 1812 changed everything. In fall 1814, British troops had stormed Washington, D.C. They had burned the capitol, the President's House, and the Library of Congress.

To the man who had always adored books, the loss of the nation's library was heartbreaking. Offering his nearly 6,500-volume collection as a new beginning, Jefferson told Congress to name its price. Congress paid $23,950 for Jefferson's books. "I cannot live without books," announced Jefferson soon after the sale, and he began to rebuild his library. Over the next ten years, he bought nearly one thousand books.

RESTORING A FRIENDSHIP

It had been more than a decade since John Adams and Thomas Jefferson had spoken. Political differences and Adams's defeat in the election of 1800 had caused a rift that no one was sure could ever be mended. Even so, Dr. Benjamin Rush had to try. Rush was a member of the Continental Congress, and he had signed the Declaration of Independence. Rush regularly wrote to Jefferson and Adams to urge them to restore their friendship, but he could not seem to get the ball rolling.

In 1811 John Adams and Thomas Jefferson rekindled their friendship after ten years of silence.

In summer 1811 Edward Coles, President Madison's aide and an Albemarle neighbor of Jefferson's, stopped at Adams's home in Quincy, Massachusetts. During their visit, Adams said, "I always loved Jefferson, and still love him." When the comment reached Jefferson, he wrote

Rush, "this is enough for me." Adams made the first move, and Jefferson wrote back. To Rush, Jefferson wrote, "I find friendship to be like wine, raw when new, ripened with age, the true old man's milk and restorative cordial." For the next fifteen years, until their deaths, Adams and Jefferson wrote more than 150 letters to one another. The former presidents shared their thoughts on science, politics, history, literature, philosophy, religion, current events, aging, and more. They kidded, debated, discussed, and posed questions:

> *Dear Sir:*
> *I cannot be serious. I am about to write You, the most frivolous letter, you ever read. Would you go back to your Cradle and live over again your 70 Years?*
>
> —John Adams to Thomas Jefferson,
> March 2, 1816

> *You ask if I would agree to live my 70 or rather 73 years over again? To which I say, Yea. I think with you, that it is a good world on the whole, that it has been framed on a principle of benevolence, and more pleasure than pain dealt out to us.*
>
> —Thomas Jefferson to John Adams,
> April 8, 1816

A LEGACY OF EDUCATION

Forty years earlier, the Virginia legislature had rejected Jefferson's plan for creating a statewide educational system. In 1817 Jefferson tried again with the Bill for Establishing a System of Public Education. It was his last big push to get Virginia to view education as a right, not a privilege. It, too, was defeated. Frustrated, Jefferson

The Thorn of Slavery

In 1814 Edward Coles wrote Jefferson with the news that he (Coles), had inherited some slaves from his father and intended on setting them free. Coles urged Jefferson to take up the banner for the abolitionist cause in Virginia "from the principles you have professed and practiced through a long and useful life." Jefferson declined, telling his neighbor that he was too old to lead the fight: "Nothing is more certainly written in the book of fate than these people are to be free; nor is it less certain that the two races, equally free, cannot live in the same government." Jefferson thought freed slaves should be sent to the American West, the Caribbean, or Africa. Coles eventually moved to Illinois, freed his slaves, and became governor of the state.

As tensions over slavery grew in the United States, the proslavery South and the antislavery North found themselves in a tug-of-war over how new states should be admitted to the union. In 1820 Congress tried to get the regions to meet halfway with the Missouri Compromise. It admitted Maine as a free state, made Missouri a slave state, and permitted slavery only in new states that formed south of an invisible dividing line at 36°30' latitude in the Louisiana Territory. This geographical division, "like a firebell in the night, awakened and filled me with terror," wrote Jefferson. He predicted a terrible struggle over the issue of slavery—one that could very well rip apart the union. The Civil War (1861–1865), the bloodiest conflict in American history, proved Jefferson right.

decided to turn his attention to an idea he had been thinking about since the early days of his presidency: a state university.

Now seventy-three years old, Jefferson had the time—and still plenty of energy—for the project. He jumped into it with both feet. Jefferson helped raise money for construction, won the approval of the state legislature, selected the site in Charlottesville, designed the campus architecture, and oversaw its construction. He created the curriculum, selected the books for the library, and hired European scholars as professors—a move to which Adams objected, saying American professors offered "more active ingenuity, and independent minds, than you can

One of Thomas Jefferson's most enduring contribution was the establishment of the University of Virginia in Charlottesville.

bring from Europe." The university was Jefferson's crowning achievement. "It is the last act of usefulness I can render," he said in 1821, "and could I see it open I would not ask an hour more of life." He got his wish. After ten years of work, Jefferson was there on March 7, 1825, to welcome the first group of sixty-eight students to the University of Virginia. Today, with an enrollment of more than 20,000 students, the University of Virginia consistently ranks among the top public universities in the nation.

Final Days

By the early 1820s Monticello was no longer generating enough income for Jefferson, his family, and his slaves to live on. Crop prices had fallen. So had land prices. Even so, Jefferson continued entertaining visitors, helping neighbors and family members, purchasing books and art, and refurbishing Monticello. He fell deeper into debt. Out of funds, Jefferson asked the state legislature to allow him to sell much of his land and belongings by lottery. This was a way of getting a fair price at a time when land prices were low. He hoped it would allow him to keep Monticello. When the news got out that Jefferson was nearly bankrupt, Americans began sending money to help. More than $16,000 came in from ordinary citizens across the nation. The generosity moved Jefferson.

In summer 1826 Jefferson was asked to attend the Fourth of July festivities in Washington, D.C. It was the fiftieth anniversary celebration of the Declaration of Independence. Sadly, Jefferson was too ill to go. He had suffered from poor health for a few years, and over the past several months he had gotten worse. In one of the last letters he wrote before his death, Jefferson had to turn down the invitation to join in the Independence Day celebration:

During Jefferson's later years he fell upon hard times and suffered from poor health.

I should, indeed, with peculiar delight, have met and exchanged there congratulations personally with the small band . . . and to have enjoyed with them the consolatory fact, that our fellow citizens, after half a century of experience and prosperity, continue to approve the choice we made."

—Thomas Jefferson, June 24, 1826

By this time the legislature had approved Jefferson's lottery request but had insisted that Monticello be included in the deal. After all, Jefferson owed creditors more than $100,000.

Perhaps it was a blessing that Jefferson did not live to see his home, property, and slaves sold to pay off his many debts. "All my wishes end, where I hope my days will end, at Monticello," Jefferson once wrote. Indeed, his days did end at home. On July 2, 1826, Jefferson fell ill with fever. He awoke several times over the next few days to ask, "Is it the Fourth of July?" After hearing that it was Independence Day, Jefferson died that afternoon at 12:50 PM. Hundreds of miles away in Quincy, Massachusetts, John Adams was barely clinging to life. At noon, he awoke to whisper, "Thomas Jefferson survives." But his old friend was already gone. Before the sun set, Adams, too, passed away. It was an eerie end that these two men, whose lives had been so closely intertwined as patriots, founding fathers, and friends, should die within hours of each other exactly fifty years after the United States adopted the Declaration of Independence.

Jefferson was buried beside his wife, Martha, at Monticello. Before his death, he had designed and written his epitaph. The plain stone pillar reads as follows:

An American Tribute

The thirty-second U.S. president, Franklin Delano Roosevelt (1882–1945), was inspired by Jefferson's contributions to democracy. He got Congress to approve $3 million to build the Thomas Jefferson National memorial along the shores of the Potomac River in Washington, D.C. Roosevelt asked that the memorial be placed in view of the White House so he could see it from his window. Designed by architect John Russell Pope, the building reflects the Roman classical style of architecture that Jefferson loved. Inside, a 19-foot bronze statue of Jefferson stands facing the White House. The white marble walls of the memorial are inscribed

with some of Jefferson's most famous quotations. The dome's rotunda features this one: "I have sworn upon the altar of God eternal hostility against every form of tyranny over the mind of man." Roosevelt dedicated the memorial on April 13, 1943, the two hundredth anniversary of Jefferson's birth.

Here was buried
Thomas Jefferson
Author of the Declaration of American Independence
Of the Statute of Virginia for Religious Freedom
And Father of the University of Virginia

Jefferson chose not to include his roles as governor, secretary of state, vice president, or president on his marker. He said that it was "by these, as testimonials that I have lived, I wish most to be remembered."

In death, as in life, Jefferson stirred up plenty of debate. Some people, like presidents Abraham Lincoln and Franklin D. Roosevelt, viewed him as a hero for defending the rights and liberties of the common man. Others saw him as a villain for excluding African Americans, American Indians, and women from that noble cause. Some applauded his stand on religious freedom, while others felt his tactics undermined religion in America. Certainly, Jefferson was a man with many sides, and we are left to ponder them all. In the final decade of his life Jefferson wrote to John Adams, "I like the dreams of the future better than the history of the past." However Americans choose to remember his legacy, words, and actions, Thomas Jefferson was, above all else, a dreamer.

As third president of the United States, Thomas Jefferson's legacy lives on today.

TIMELINE

1743
Born April 13 near Charlottesville, Virginia

1760–1762
Attended the College of William and Mary

1769–1775
Served in the Virginia House of Burgesses

1772
Marries Martha Wayles Skelton

1775
Elected Virginia delegate to the Second Continental Congress

1776
Wrote the Declaration of Independence

1779–1781
Served as governor of Virginia

1740

1784–1789
Served as ambassador
to France

1790–1793
Appointed first U.S.
secretary of state

1797–1801
Served as vice president
of the United States

1801–1805
Served first term as
president of the
United States

1805–1809
Served second
presidential term

1826
Died July 4, on the
fiftieth anniversary of
the Declaration of
Independence

1830

NOTES

CHAPTER 1

p. 7, "Life, liberty . . ." : The Declaration of Independence, The National Archives Experience, The U.S. National Archives and Records Administration, www.archives.gov/national-archivesexperience/charters/declaration_transcript.html (accessed February 7, 2008).

p. 7, The Declaration was recently ranked . . . : The People's Vote, sponsored by the U.S. National Archives, National History Day, and *U.S News & World Report*, www.ourdocuments.gov (accessed October 15, 2007).

p. 7, "knowledge is power . . .": Noble E. Cunningham Jr. *In Pursuit of Reason: The Life of Thomas Jefferson* (New York: Random House, 1987), xiii.

p. 8, ". . . make the first map of Virginia . . .": Thomas Jefferson, *The Life and Selected Writings of Thomas Jefferson*, ed. Adrienne Koch and William Peden (New York: Random House, 1993), 8.

p. 9, "My father's education . . .": Jefferson, *The Life and Selected Writings*, 7.

p. 10, "When I recollect . . ." : Jefferson to Thomas Randolph Jefferson, 24 November 1808, in *The Life and Selected Writings*, 540.

p. 13, "I am savage enough . . .": Jefferson to Baron Geismer, 6 September 1785, in *The Life and Selected Writings*, 353.

p. 14, Monticello Facts: The Thomas Jefferson Foundation, www.monticello.org; UNESCO World Heritage Center, http://whc.unesco.org.

p. 15, ". . . every paper I had in the world . . .": Cunningham Jr. *In Pursuit of Reason*, 17.

CHAPTER 2

p. 16, "[I] heard the splendid display . . .": Jefferson, *The Life and Selected Writings*, 10.

p. 16, ". . . the laziest man in reading . . .": Jefferson, *The Life and Selected Writings*, 14.

p. 18, "Taxation without representation . . .": www.quotationspage.com/quotes /James_Otis/.

p. 18, ". . . in all cases whatsoever.": 6 George III, c. 12, *The Statutes at Large*, ed. Danby Pickering (London, 1767), XXVII, 19–20, The Constitution Society, www.constitution.org/bcp/decl_act.htm (accessed October 15, 2007).

p. 20, ". . . a very attractive person . . .": The Thomas Jefferson Foundation, Martha Wayles Skelton Jefferson, http://wiki.monticello.org/mediawiki/index.php/Martha _Wayles_Skelton_Jefferson (accessed October 29, 2007).

p. 20, ". . . the greatest fund . . .": Cunningham Jr., *In Pursuit of Reason*, 21.

p. 20, ". . . unchequered happiness.": Jefferson, *The Life and Selected Writings*, 51.

p. 21, ". . . a day of fasting, humiliation, and prayer . . .": Jefferson, *The Life and Selected Writings*, 12.

p. 22, ". . . the British Parliament has no right . . .": Jefferson, *The Life and Selected Writings*, 277, 288–289.

p. 23, "Mr. Jefferson had the Reputation . . .": Cunningham Jr., *In Pursuit of Reason*, 31.

p. 24, ". . . and by the Pamphlet . . .": Cunningham Jr., *In Pursuit of Reason*, 36.

p. 24, "During the whole time . . .": John Adams, *The Works of John Adams*, ed. Charles Francis Adams (Boson, MA: 1856), Vol. II, 513–514.

p. 24, ". . . traitorous correspondence . . .": R. B. Bernstein, *Thomas Jefferson* (New York: Oxford University Press, 2003), 27.

p. 25, ". . . unanimously pressed on myself alone . . ." : Bernstein, *Thomas Jefferson*, 32.

p. 26, Did You Know? facts: The National Archives, www.archives.gov.

p. 27, ". . . We hold these truths . . .": The Declaration of Independence, The National Archives Experience, The U.S. National Archives and Records Administration, www.archives.gov/national-archivesexperience/charters/declaration_transcript .html (accessed February 7, 2008).

p. 27, "I was sitting by Dr. Franklin . . .": Walter Isaacson, "Benjamin Franklin Joins the Revolution," Smithsonian.com, August 1, 2003, www.smithsonianmag.com/ history-archaeology/10010281.html (accessed February 7, 2008).

p. 28, "He has waged cruel war . . .": Jefferson, *The Life and Selected Writings*, 26.

p. 28, ". . . an abominable crime . . .": Jefferson and Slavery, Getting Word: African Americans at Monticello, The Thomas Jefferson Foundation, www.monticello .org/gettingword/views.html (accessed October 23, 2007).

CHAPTER 3

p. 30, ". . . without regard to wealth . . .": Cunningham Jr., *In Pursuit of Reason*, 60.

p. 32, "The legitimate powers . . .": Jefferson, "Notes on Virginia," in *The Life and Selected Writings*, 254.

p. 32, "My opinion is that . . .": *Thomas Jefferson*, producers Ken Burns and Camilla Rockwell, 180 min., PBS Home Video, 1997, DVD.

p. 33, ". . . no man shall be compelled . . .": Thomas Jefferson, "The Virginia Act for Establishing Religious Freedom," The Founders' Constitution, ed. Philip B. Kurland and Ralph Lerner, University of Chicago Press, http://press-pubs.uchicago.edu (accessed November 6, 2007).

p. 33, ". . . destroys the morals . . ." : Jefferson, "Notes on Virginia," in *The Life and Selected Writings*, 257.

p. 34, "Nothing would induce me . . .": The Thomas Jefferson Foundation, "A Day in the Life: To Labour For Another," www.monticello.org/jefferson/dayinlife/ plantation/dig.html (accessed October 23, 2007).

p. 35, "But as it is, we have the wolf . . .": Jefferson to John Holms, 22 April 1820, in *The Life and Selected Writings*, 637.

p. 36, ". . . unprepared by his line . . .": Cunningham Jr., *In Pursuit of Reason*, 71.

p. 37, ". . . perfectly tranquil . . .": Gaye Wilson, "A Narrow Escape from the British Thanks to Jack Jouett," The Thomas Jefferson Foundation, Monticello Newsletter, Vol. 17, No. 2, Winter 2006.

p. 37, ". . . for his impartial, upright . . .": Cunningham Jr., *In Pursuit of Reason*, 74.

p. 37, "I have taken my final leave . . .": *Thomas Jefferson*, PBS Home Video, DVD.

p. 39, ". . . so amiable, . . .": Lester J. Cappon, editor, *The Adams-Jefferson Letters: The Complete Correspondence Between Thomas Jefferson and Abigail and John Adams* (Chapel Hill: University of North Carolina Press, 1987), xxxvi.

p. 40, ". . . wiped away all my plans . . .": Jefferson to Francois Jean, Chevalier de Chastellux, 26 November 1782, in *The Life and Selected Writings*, 340.

p. 40, "And in those melancholy rambles . . .": *Thomas Jefferson*, PBS Home Video, DVD.

Chapter 4

p. 44, "If anybody thinks . . .": Jefferson to George Wythe, 13 August 1786, in *The Life and Selected Writings*, 366.

p. 47, *"Head. Well, friend, . . ."*: Jefferson to Maria Cosway, 12 October 1786, *The Life and Selected Writings*, 367.

p. 47, "I hold it, that a little rebellion,. . .": Jefferson to James Madison, 30 January 1787, *The Life and Selected Writings*, 383.

p. 48, ". . . freedom of religion . . .": Jefferson to James Madison, 20 December 1787, *The Life and Selected Writings*, 404.

p. 50, "The people. . . ": The Treasury Building: Online Exhibit," The Office of Curator, Department of Treasury, 2002, www.treas.gov/offices/management/curator/exhibitions/2002exhibit/print_secretary.html (accessed November 16, 2007).

p. 52, "Hamilton was . . . so bewitched . . .": Jefferson, *The Life and Selected Writings*, 117.

p. 52, ". . . to make all laws . . .": U.S. Constitution, Article I, Sec. 8, 1788, The National Archives, www.archives.gov/exhibits/charters/constitution_transcript.html (accessed November 12, 2007).

p. 53, "My earnest wish . . .": Bernstein, *Thomas Jefferson*, 98.

p. 55, "It requires no talent . . .": Philadelphia *Aurora*, September 20, 1796, (New York: Oxford University Press, 2003), 113.

Chapter 5

p. 59, "His dress was, as usual, . . .": Cunningham Jr., *In Pursuit of Reason*, 238.

p. 61, "Let us, then, fellow-citizens, . . .": Jefferson's Inauguration Address, 4 March 1801, *The Life and Selected Writings*, 298.

p. 61, ". . . among Rotten Apples.": Susan Dunn, *Jefferson's Second Revolution: The Election Crisis of 1800 and the Triumph of Republicanism* (Boston: Houghton Mifflin, 2004), 8.

p. 62, ". . . bankrupt beyond redemption.": Dunn, *Jefferson's Second Revolution*, 202.

p. 64, ". . . the revolution of 1800, . . .": James Horn, "Jefferson and the Revolution of 1800," Monticello Newsletter, Vol. 11, No. 1, Spring 2000.

p. 68, "The territory acquired . . .": Jefferson to Horatio Gates, 11 July 1803, in *The Life and Selected Writings*, 523.

p. 69, "Her name is Sally. . . ": James T. Callender, *Richmond Recorder*, September 1, 1802, www.pbs.org/jefferson/archives/documents/ih195822z.htm (accessed February 1, 2008).

Chapter 6

p. 71, ". . . a rising nation, . . .": Jefferson, *The Life and Selected Writings*, 297.

p. 73, ". . . in body and mind equal . . .": Jefferson to Francois Jean, Chevalier de Chastellux, 7 June 1785, in "Thomas Jefferson's Enlightenment and American Indians," the Thomas Jefferson Foundation, www.monticello.org/jefferson/lewisandclark/enlightenindian.html (accessed December 18, 2007).

p. 74, ". . . blot in our moral history . . .": 18 July 1824, "Slavery and Thomas Jefferson Quotations," the Thomas Jefferson Foundation, www.monticello.org/gettingword/slaveryquos.html (accessed February 9, 2008).

p. 74, "brave, prudent, habituated to the woods . . .": Irving W. Anderson, "Captain Meriwether Lewis," Inside the Corps, PBS, www.pbs.org/lewisandclark/inside/mlewi.html (accessed February 6, 2008).

p. 75, "In all your intercourse with the natives . . .": "Jefferson's Instructions to Meriwether Lewis," the Thomas Jefferson Foundation, www.monticello.org/jefferson/lewisandclark/instructions.html (accessed December 12, 2007).

p. 75, ". . . unspeakable joy, . . .": "Thomas Jefferson, President of the United States: Kingly Over Republican Government," the Thomas Jefferson Foundation, http://classroom.monticello.org/teachers/resources/profile/264/Thomas-Jefferson-President-of-the-United-States (accessed February 2, 2008).

p. 76, ". . . I . . . have lost . . .": Katherine. G. Revell, "Thomas Jefferson: A Day in the Life," the Thomas Jefferson Foundation, www.monticello.org/jefferson/dayinlife/breakfast/profile.html#maria (accessed November 12, 2007).

p. 79, "We have traitors . . .": Cunningham Jr., *In Pursuit of Reason*, 286.

p. 79, "Yet although there is not a man . . .": Jefferson to Monsieur DuPont de Nemours, 14 July 1807, in *The Life and Selected Writings*, 536.

p. 80, "This country has never . . .": Jefferson to James Bowdoin, 10 July 1807, in *The Writings of Thomas Jefferson*, ed. Paul Leicester Ford (New York: G. P. Putman's sons, 1892–99), Vol. 9: 109.

p. 82, "Our ships all in motion . . .": John M. Murrin, "The Jeffersonian Triumph and American Exceptionalism," *Journal of the Early Republic* (Indianapolis: Spring 2000), http://access-proxy.sno-isle.org/login?url=http://proquest.umi.com.access-proxy.sno-isle.org/pqdweb?did=56380780&Fmt=7&clientId=19740&RQT=309&VName=PQD (accessed February 1, 2008).

p. 82, "Within a few days I retire . . .": Jefferson to Monsieur DuPont de Nemours, 2 March 1809, in *The Life and Selected Writings*, 545.

p. 83, "Mr. Jefferson appeared . . .": Cunningham Jr., *In Pursuit of Reason*, 319.

Chapter 7

p. 85, "My mornings are devoted . . .": Jefferson to Thaddeus Kosciusko, 26 February 1810, in *The Life and Selected Writings*, 552.

p. 86, "I cannot live without books . . .": Cunningham Jr., *In Pursuit of Reason*, 333.

p. 86, ". . . I always loved Jefferson, . . .": Cappon, *The Adams-Jefferson Letters*, 284.

p. 87, ". . . this is enough for me.": "Jefferson and Adams: A Lifetime of Letters," the Thomas Jefferson Foundation, www.monticello.org/jefferson/dayinlife/cabinet/profile.html (accessed February 1, 2008).

p. 87, ". . . I find friendship . . .": Jefferson to Benjamin Rush, 17 August 1811, in *The Life and Selected Writings*, 563.

p. 87, "Dear Sir: . . .": Cappon, *The Adams-Jefferson Letters*, 464–467.

p. 88, ". . . from the principles . . .": Cunningham, *In Pursuit of Reason*, 348.

p. 88, ". . . Nothing is more certainly written . . .": Jefferson, *The Life and Selected Writings*, 49.

p. 88, ". . . awakened and filled me . . .": Jefferson to John Holmes, 22 April 1820, in *The Life and Selected Writings*, 637.

p. 90, ". . . more active ingenuity, . . .": Adams to Jefferson, 22 January 1825, in *The Adams-Jefferson Letters*, 607.

p. 90, "It is the last act . . .": "Quotations on the University of Virginia," the Thomas Jefferson Foundation, http://wiki.monticello.org/mediawiki/index.php/Quotations_on_the_University_of_Virginia (accessed February 2, 2008).

p. 90, "Today, with an enrollment of . . .": "America Best Colleges: 2008," *U.S. News and World Report*, http://colleges.usnews.rankingsandreviews.com/usnews/edu/college/rankings/brief/natudoc_pub_brief.php (accessed February 2, 2008).

p. 92, "I should, indeed, with peculiar delight, . . .": Jefferson to Roger C. Weightman, 24 June 1826, in *The Life and Selected Writings*, 666.

p. 92, "All my wishes end, . . .": "A Day in the Life of Thomas Jefferson: All My Wishes End," the Thomas Jefferson Foundation," www.monticello.org/jefferson/dayinlife/wishes/home.html (accessed December 14, 2007).

p. 92, ". . . Thomas Jefferson survives.": "Jefferson and Adams: A Lifetime of Letters," the Thomas Jefferson Foundation, www.monticello.org/jefferson/dayinlife/cabinet/profile.html (accessed January 13, 2008).

p. 93, ". . . I have sworn upon the altar . . .": Jefferson to Benjamin Rush, 1800, in "Thomas Jefferson on Politics and Government: Quotations from the Writings of Thomas Jefferson," University of Virginia, http://etext.virginia.edu/jefferson/quotations/index.htm (accessed January 15, 2008); Thomas Jefferson Memorial, www.thedistrict.com/placestogo/monumentsmemorials/jeffersonmemorial.html

p. 94, "Here was buried . . .": "A Day in the Life of Thomas Jefferson: All My Wishes End," the Thomas Jefferson Foundation, www.monticello.org/jefferson/dayinlife/wishes/home.html (accessed January 14, 2008).

p. 94, ". . . by these, as testimonials . . .": Cunningham Jr., *In Pursuit of Reason*, 349.

p. 94, ". . . I like the dreams of the future . . .": Jefferson to John Adams, 1 August 1816, in *The Life and Selected Writings*, 618.

GLOSSARY

boycott a pledge to stop doing business with an individual, company, or government out of protest

cede to surrender land rights

deserted left the military without permission, intending not to return

embargo a government order that prohibits merchant ships from entering or leaving its ports

impressments acts of unlawfully seizing people and forcing them into public service

manumission the act of freeing someone from slavery

militia a reserve army made up of civilians that is often called upon to serve with regular forces in an emergency

monarchy a system of government in which someone, such as a king or queen, rules a territory for life, often by hereditary right

Parliament the legislative body of Britain

primogeniture a traditional English law requiring that upon the death of an adult male, the bulk of his holdings and property go to the eldest son

repeal to cancel a law

surveyor someone who takes measurements of land areas to determine boundaries, elevations, and dimensions

tyranny the cruel use of power by a person or government to control others

veto the power of one branch of legislative government to reject the legislation of another.

Further Information

Books

Behrman, Carol H. *Thomas Jefferson*. Minneapolis, MN: Lerner Publications, 2006.

Davis, Kenneth. *Don't Know Much About Thomas Jefferson*. New York: HarperCollins, 2005.

Elish, Dan. *James Madison*. New York: Marshall Cavendish Benchmark, 2008.

Nelson, Sheila. *Thomas Jefferson's America: The Louisiana Purchase 1800–1811*. Philadelphia: Mason Crest Publishers, 2005.

Pflueger, Lynda. *Thomas Jefferson: Creating a Nation*. Berkeley Heights, NJ: Enslow Publishers, 2004.

Stewart, Mark. *The Indian Removal Act: A Forced Relocation*. Minneapolis, MN: Compass Point Books, 2007.

DVDs

Thomas Jefferson: The Private Man, The Public Figure. Empire for Liberty.

Thomas Jefferson: A Film by Ken Burns. PBS Home Video.

WEB SITES

Monticello: Home of Thomas Jefferson

http://monticello.org

Log on to discover more about Thomas Jefferson's life, family, home, and politics. "Ask Thomas Jefferson" a question, take a tour of Monticello online, or plan your visit to Monticello.

Library of Congress: Thomas Jefferson

www.loc.gov/exhibits/jefferson

Explore the achievements of the third president of the United States, from the Declaration of Independence to the Lewis and Clark expedition. The Library of Congress is home to the *Thomas Jefferson Papers*, the largest collection of original Jefferson documents in the world.

The White House

www.whitehouse.gov/history/presidents/tj3.html

Read a brief history of Thomas Jefferson and other U.S. presidents at the official White House Web site.

BIBLIOGRAPHY

Bernstein, R. B. *Thomas Jefferson*. New York: Oxford University Press, 2003.

Cappon, Lester J., editor. *The Adams-Jefferson Letters: The Complete Correspondence Between Thomas Jefferson and Abigail and John Adams*. Chapel Hill: University of North Carolina Press, 1998.

Crawford, Alan Pell. *Twilight at Monticello: The Final Years of Thomas Jefferson*. New York: Random House, 2008.

Cunningham, Noble E. Jr. *In Pursuit of Reason: The Life of Thomas Jefferson*. New York: Random House, 1987.

Dunn, Susan. *Jefferson's Second Revolution: The Election Crisis of 1800 and the Triumph of Republicanism*. Boston: Houghton Mifflin, 2004.

Halliday, E. M. *Understanding Thomas Jefferson*. New York: Harper-Collins, 2001.

Hitchens, Christopher. *Thomas Jefferson: Author of America*. Waterville, ME: Thorndike Press, 2005.

Jefferson, Thomas. *The Life and Selected Writings of Thomas Jefferson*. Edited by Adrienne Koch and William Peden. New York: Random House, 1993.

———. *Light and Liberty: Reflections on the Pursuit of Happiness*. Edited by Eric. S. Petersen. New York: Random House, 2004.

Stanton, Lucia. *Free Some Day: The African-American Families of Monticello*. Charlottesville, VA: The Thomas Jefferson Foundation, 2000.

INDEX

Pages in **boldface** are illustrations.

Hamilton, Alexander, 50, **51**, 52, 56, 62, 78, **78**
Hemings, Sally, 69
Henry, Patrick, 16, **17**, 44, 48

impressment, 80, **81**

Jefferson, Jane (daughter), 30
Jefferson, Jane (mother), 8, 14
Jefferson, Lucy (daughter), 38, 40, 42
Jefferson, Maria (daughter), 40, 42, 76
Jefferson, Martha "Patsy" (daughter), 20, 40, 42, 50, 76
Jefferson, Martha (wife), 19–20, 38, 40, 92
Jefferson, Peter (father), 8, 9–10, 12
Jefferson, Thomas, **6**, **27**, **39**, **45**, **49**, **57**, **60**, **72**, **77**, **91**, **95**
   autobiography of, 9
   Bill of Rights and, 48
   birth of, 8
   childhood of, 8
   Constitution and, 41, 48, 52, 55, 70
   death of, 92, 94
   debt of, 85, 90, 92
   Declaration of Independence and, 25, 27–28, **27**, 92
   education and, 30–31, 39, 87, 89–90, **89**, 94
   education of, 7, 9, **9**, 10, 11, **11**, 15
   elections of, 10, 19, 30, 35, 55–56, 61–64, 76, 86
   Embargo Act and, 80–82
   Enlightenment and, 12, 27, 30, 32, 50
   as governor of Virginia, 35, 36, 37, 55–56
   health of, 46, 90, **91**
   in House of Burgesses, 15, 16, 19, 20, 21
   in House of Delegates, 30–31, 31–33, 33–35

ABOUT THE AUTHOR

An award-winning broadcast journalist, Trudi Strain Trueit has written more than forty fiction and nonfiction books for children on weather, wildlife, earth science, health, and history (her favorite!). For Marshall Cavendish Benchmark, she has written Benchmark Rebus Creepy Critters and Weather Watch series. She has a BA in Broadcast Journalism from Pacific Lutheran University in Tacoma, Washington. Trudi was born and raised near Seattle. She still lives in the Pacific Northwest with her husband, Bill, a high school photography teacher. You can read more about her and her books at www.truditrueit.com.